Stopping the Brain Drain of Skilled Veteran Teachers

Stopping the Brain Drain of Skilled Veteran Teachers

Retaining and Valuing Their Hard-Won Experience

William L. Fibkins

ROWMAN & LITTLEFIELD EDUCATION

A division of

ROWMAN & LITTLEFIELD PUBLISHERS, INC.
Lanham • New York • Toronto • Plymouth, UK

Published by Rowman & Littlefield Education
A division of Rowman & Littlefield Publishers, Inc.
A wholly owned subsidiary of The Rowman & Littlefield Publishing Group, Inc.
4501 Forbes Boulevard, Suite 200, Lanham, Maryland 20706
http://www.rowmaneducation.com

Estover Road, Plymouth PL6 7PY, United Kingdom

British Library Cataloguing in Publication Information Available

Library of Congress Cataloging-in-Publication Data Available

ISBN 978-1-61048-336-0 (cloth : alk. paper)
ISBN 978-1-61048-337-7 (paper : alk. paper)
ISBN 978-1-61048-338-4 (electronic)

∞™ The paper used in this publication meets the minimum requirements of American National Standard for Information Sciences—Permanence of Paper for Printed Library Materials, ANSI/NISO Z39.48-1992.

Printed in the United States of America

Dedication

This book is dedicated to Suzanne Jones. Sue has served as my typist, editor, critic, and chief supporter in preparing all my books for publication. She has been *the* major force in helping me move my publications across the goal line. Sue has a special skill to clarify my ideas and words and make them more interesting and compelling for the reader. And she has the ability to stand tough and be a needed critic; meet pressured deadlines; work very hard; and, most of the time, keep a smile on her face. However, being human, she can deliver a needed wake-up call when my so-called "creative" side gets in the way and becomes problematic. Sue is a good steward and is able to keep divergent people like me focused when the train begins leaving the track.

Clearly I would not be the successful writer I have become without her guidance. I would not be able to share my ideas with educators who care deeply, as Sue and I do, about children, educators, and parents who find themselves heading toward the margins of school and community unless they are given the intervention, care, and support they desperately need.

Sue understands the cries of children, adults, and families for support. Her full-time job involves facilitating help for individuals and families caught in the legal system, prisoners, released prisoners, and their families. She has witnessed families being destroyed because they found themselves in the wrong place at the wrong time and without needed resources and advocates to show them the way.

Our work as advocates for those in need has forged a bond with the mission of creating many open doors of help for students in school and for families at risk in the community. Every writer needs a "Sue," not only for manuscript prep, but also to bring home to the writer the need to tell the real story about what it means to be at risk and how important it is to have teachers in your corner who are willing and skilled at helping, teachers who don't look the other way when they observe pain in the eyes of their students. Rather, they act and stand by students as they begin the road away from problematic lives.

William L. Fibkins

Contents

Foreword

The challenges facing American schools have changed considerably over the last two decades, in ways that today's grandparents probably do not recognize. Consider this:

1. Unmarried women account for 40 percent of all live births in the United States today. Thus, chances are that a good number of rising kindergartners and children in lower grades arrive lacking basic discipline training, and may not have enjoyed such things as being read aloud to before bed and so forth, as their exhausted single moms struggle to cope.
2. Independent of the above statistic, one in ten primary and secondary school students are not native English speakers—instead, they struggle through class using English as a second language, often not spoken at home.
3. At least in part contributed to by the above statistics, only two of every three high school students graduate in the "normal" four years.

Imagine an army faced with a battle—and on the eve of the battle, all the seasoned veterans went to have a quiet drink, and share a pizza—which was bad. They all got so sick they could not mentor the new recruits, provide steady leadership borne of experience, and pitch in wherever needed. What do you think the outcome of the battle would be?

If ever there is a case for the need to keep and benefit from experienced, high-performing teachers, these three statistics say it all.

And now the kicker: Many school systems are focusing on cutting the most experienced teachers from their payroll because of the higher rate of pay their experience costs the system. Or they encourage early retirement. So, just when we need the most experienced teachers, we are sending in raw recruits instead. Into this challenge of larger classes of single-parent students, many of whom do not speak English well, we throw young, inexperienced teaches who flee in droves after a year or two.

Bill Fibkins provides a plan to create career alternatives for highly skilled veteran teachers who want to remain on board as full-time or part-time mentors and trainers and not retire. This is a needed intervention to insure stability, particularly for our large secondary schools, given the increasing number of novice teacher now filling our classrooms. A sound public policy requires that we stop the brain drain of our best senior teachers and act to avoid leaving our schools to be led by inexperienced educators—a prescription for chaos and crisis making.

There are many ways we can shape our future—we are not powerless. And Dr. Fibkins shows us one more place we can put the lever to move the world in a better direction.

Francis Koster Ed.D.
President
The Optimistic Futurist

Chapter 1

The Loss of Skilled Veteran Teachers

Is It a Problem of Our Outdated Policy and Practice?

In chapter 7 of the second edition of *An Administrator's Guide to Better Teacher Mentoring*,[1] I suggested that experienced teachers are needed as models and mentors for the large number of novice teachers entering the profession. Without the intervention and training offered by veteran teachers, many novice teachers will experience failure and exit the profession, a loss that can be averted by involving teachers who have hard-earned classroom experience in guiding beginning teachers through the pitfalls that emerge not only with students in the classroom but also in relationships with peers, administrators, parents and community members. These are constituencies that can be equally risky for novices who have yet to learn the dark side of school and community life and politics.

There is a steep learning curve for well-intentioned but often naive beginners that can be successfully bridged with the help of veteran teachers who know the school culture and are committed to serving as big brother, big sister, mentor, model, quasi therapist, coach, and friend. This is a much-needed role in our schools.

However, as I point out in this book, there are major roadblocks to enlisting veteran teachers in this needed process that go beyond selling them on this new role and providing the needed training to be successful models and mentors.

In America today there is a major effort by leaders in business, industry, government and the professions to reduce the number of aging employees by offering perks such as early retirement incentives. In the education community veteran teachers are being wooed with cash buyouts, quickly offered, often without much time to consider the impact on their professional and personal lives or the support resources to help them navigate this crucial decision whether to stay or leave. The current economic climate is giving rise to a nationwide buyout of veteran, high-earning teachers to make room for inexperienced, unskilled, and low-earning novice teachers.

What we are observing in almost every work setting in America, including education, is a fast-exit process for many skilled employees, leaving behind a workforce made up of workers who are not only inexperienced and unskilled but often have few experienced mentors and models to turn to for guidance, advice, support, and know-how. As a result, in our education community there is a growing shortage of skilled veteran teachers just at the time they are needed most. Clearly many novice teachers are not going to survive given the increasing lack of veteran teachers to pass on their experience and wisdom.

This fast-exit process also includes successful school building and district administrators who are caught up in the same "discard fever." The days are over when a new principal came to town as a young man or woman, became a pillar of the community, and stayed at the helm until illness or death. There are few building principals like George Forbes, whom I describe in the second edition of *An Administrator's Guide to Better Teacher Mentoring*,[2] homegrown administrators who work their way up through the ranks to leadership positions.

Forbes's career in the Bay Shore, New York, public schools spanned over forty years. He served as counselor, school psychologist, and principal at Bay Shore Junior High School and left on his own terms because of ill health. His was a career model that was common practice for administrators until the turbulent days of the 1980s when our schools became the focus of citizen anger because of student rebellion, budget concerns, and poor student achievement. School administrators became the targets for angry citizens and were the first to go, often the scapegoats, taking the rap for events beyond their control.

The 1980s gave rise to our current buyout mentality, beginning a negative cycle in many school districts of administrators serving short periods of time until they were booted or bought out, a revolving door that led to a lack of continuity in leadership. As a result, in today's world and particularly in our large secondary schools, the tenure of administrators no longer resembles that of George Forbes, who stayed in one place; knew his students, teachers, and community; and had a cadre of community leaders to watch his back when the attacks came.

The buyout of administrators, then, is a recent phenomenon that has served to make the role of building and central officer administrators even more risky and to raise the question, "Why would any successful educator want to take on a role that offers so little security?"

The early retirement of veteran teachers and administrator turnover are decimating our schools' leadership personnel. When veteran teachers and administrators exit, they take with them skills that are much needed to run a successful school.

There is a brain drain that results in inexperienced teachers and administrators being chosen for leadership roles without the experience to do the job well. Just when skilled and successful veteran teachers are needed to lead mentoring programs for novice teachers, their numbers are being reduced by ill-advised early retirement programs, programs that offer no alternatives to encourage successful veteran teachers to remain on board in creative part-time positions such as mentoring.

While it is true that one of the primary reasons for this fast-exit process has been a troubled economy, I believe there is a more subtle and disturbing process involved. Some school districts have used the troubled economy as a backdrop to implement a strategy to get rid of veteran teachers and administrators even when their financial situation doesn't warrant such a widespread process. This strategy is often applauded in the district's public relations releases as a success story, boasting that educators get bonuses to leave and new staff are hired at half or quarter of the cost.

What is missing in this "success story" is information about the skills, experience, and know-how of the educators about to leave and what a gap their leaving will cause, a gap that cannot be filled for years to come.

It is hardly a "success story." Rather it is a cover-up of a great loss to school resources. It might better be titled "the true story of losing our best and brightest veteran teachers." It is an all-too-common story in which parents and community members have been convinced that this fast-exit process is a good deal and a necessary strategy in our tough economic times. Veteran teachers and administrators have been sold on this fast-exit process because it puts a few extra dollars in their pockets. The process is akin to the captain and senior officers of an aircraft carrier voluntarily jumping overboard and leaving the crew to figure out how to run the ship.

At first this loss is not easily assessed or quantified. When someone dies it often takes a long period of grieving for us to realize just how much that person meant to us and how much we lost by his or her death. The same is true for the loss of skilled educators. At first the downside of their loss isn't apparent. You know the thinking—"People are replaceable and interchangeable." But students and involved parents and community members soon learn the hard truth, that "replacing" an experienced educator who knows the school culture, students, parents, and community usually doesn't just happen.

There are serious consequences for the education community. For example, many students returning to school after summer recess find that some of their favorite veteran teachers have suddenly disappeared and been replaced by, as one parent told me, "a bunch of inexperienced kids just out of college."

Ageism—the ideas, attitudes, rules or practices that take advantage of older people—is also a contributing factor in the fast exit of veteran teachers. The antipathy that some novice and mid-career teachers feel toward veteran teachers goes beyond fears of being laid off if the vets don't take a buyout package. It arises, as Robert Butler, the pioneering gerontologist suggests, "from deeply human concerns and fears about the vulnerability inherent in later life."[3]

After all, much of school life is focused on the young—students, parents and novice teachers who arrive fresh with enthusiasm. The culture of the school community is simply not accustomed to having older staff remain on board after retirement age, no matter how skilled they are. Older teachers are expected to exit when, as one teacher told me, "their time comes." Otherwise they risk stereotypes and labels that, as Butler suggests, "do not seem to approach the iniquity of racial epithets but in polite circles, milder terms hurt more." Maybe this kind of stereotyping doesn't rise to a charge of age discrimination but it serves to guide the conversation.

According to Butler this kind of ageism is expressed in the everyday language used to describe old people. In today's school culture older, veteran teachers are sometimes referred to in less than positive terms:—"When is she going to retire?" "He's over the hill." "She needs to be put out to pasture." "He's toast, burned out." "Just a crotchety old man (or woman)." They're "senile" "old goats" with "one foot in the grave." Maybe this type of stereotyping doesn't always rise to a charge of age discrimination, but it serves to rule the conversation in school faculty rooms about who should stay and who should go in tough economic times.

Maggie Kuhn, founder of the Gray Panthers, said, "Only the newest model is desirable. The old are condemned to obsolescence: left to rot like wrinkled babies in glorified playpens, forced to succumb to a trivial, purposeless waste of their years and their time."[4] Kuhn's comment clearly spells out the potential dark side of the "out with old, in with the new" scenario.

It's about more than job security. It's about providing a place for some veteran teachers who don't want to retire, rot and be condemned to obsolescence. It's about the need to change the school culture to make room for skilled veteran teachers who want to work, have many skills to offer and are in sync with the school's "culture of the young."

As I describe in chapters 3 and 4, people are living longer and many are choosing to work longer because they are healthy and want to contribute. Schools are going to have to find ways to accommodate older teachers, not scapegoat and stereotype them as useless baggage. The current model of "out with the old, in with the new" is slowly giving way, replaced with a "freedom to work" model rather than the "freedom not to work" model.

For school administrators the fast exit of veteran teachers is cause for alarm—alarm that the deft hand of veteran teachers in disciplining difficult students is no longer available, alarm that the ongoing effort to raise achievement levels and test scores of students will probably suffer a serious setback with veteran teachers no longer on the job, alarm that staff morale will decline now that the positive, reasoned, and experienced voices of veteran teacher leaders is silenced, and alarm that the idea of early buyouts is propelling, persuading (pushing may be a better word) teachers to focus on getting out early rather than seeing their careers develop into "master teacher" status where they can teach students as well as train novices and mid-career colleagues.

It's a process that devalues the successful experience of gifted veteran teachers by telling them, "Your time is up. Hit the road, Jack, and never look back." The person selling them on hitting the road is often the building administrator, the messenger with the task of, putting it crudely, getting rid of many of his favorite and much-needed colleagues.

In this fast exit, buyout process, building administrators are caught in an untenable, no-win position. They can't stop this negative process or support it politically, yet they are left with a school staff less prepared for what the parents and community want—well disciplined, high-achieving students, a safe school and a caring student-centered staff. No wonder that the tenure of many school administrators, particularly at the secondary level, doesn't last long. We are cutting off their legs and asking them to run a marathon.

Clearly then, it doesn't take a rocket scientist to recognize that the political risks that accompany the job of administrator often get heightened in this fast-exit process as student discipline and achievement levels falter due to an inexperienced crew of new teachers. Parents and community members may say they want to save money by buying out veteran teachers, but they are often unaware of the negative consequences of their pleas, such as creating an unruly school campus, poor student achievement, a decline in staff morale and the erosion of a successful school culture. The negative results of these buyouts often come home to roost within a short period of time but the damage has been done; there is no going back.

This is not to say that every veteran educator is looking for an alternative in order to remain a contributor to the education process, nor is every veteran teacher highly skilled or gifted. Some teachers have experienced a career in which they got by, did what they needed to do to survive. Teaching was a chore, not a rewarding experience, for them or their students. These teachers are ready for a fast exit and an early retirement buyout makes sense.

The educators who are the focus of this book are different. They are usually energetic, highly skilled, creative and at the top of their game even as they near retirement age. Many of these teachers do not see themselves as ready to retire. Why should we kick these valuable educators out the door when they can still contribute at a high level? It makes no sense to paint all educators with the same brush by offering a buyout and a fast exit to every educator, regardless of their individual skills and talents.

The majority of mediocre teachers want out because they've had limited success and many failures. The story of gifted, highly skilled veteran educators is different. They've worked hard, found the key to success, and are in no hurry to give up a career that has been and continues to be rewarding. We need to find ways to retain our most talented teachers and let the mediocre ones go gladly. As the saying goes, let's not "throw the baby out with the bath water."

We need to change this fast-exit process for all concerned—the veteran educators, their younger colleagues who will one day encounter the same dilemma, students, parents, and community members. There is a saying that "you get what you pay for." Paying less may at first seem like a bargain but over time the product may not be durable when tested in real life.

We must educate successful veteran teachers and administrators that they are much needed and instruct/counsel/guide them to assess early retirement buyouts before making a decision. Giving up a successful teaching or administrative role in order to retire can be a destructive career choice. Retirement is not always what we imagine it will be. In my conversations with retired teachers and administrators, many report that in spite of more leisure time, new activities and what appeared at first to be rewarding part-time work, they miss teaching and supervising. They miss the classroom, students, colleagues, faculty room conversation, camaraderie, school dances and football games, turbulence, excitement, and dealing with the unknown that are so much a part of our large secondary schools.

As one former high school social studies teacher told me,

I'd go back to my old classroom in a heartbeat. I'm teaching part-time in a community college and the students are zombies, uninterested, boring. I miss my high school kids, even the ball breakers. They were exciting because they constantly test you, and it's your battle to win them over. It was never dull. Sure, I have more time to travel, play golf, and all that stuff, but I sense I have become dull myself and have less hope and optimism. Since leaving my classroom I no longer need to be up and energetic, ready and set for whatever comes my way. Now not much is required of me. And I'm not alone. I go to a monthly retirement luncheon with some old buddies and they say the same thing. I think I was caught off guard with the retirement package and didn't realize what I was giving up. Many of the people at the retirement luncheon say the same thing. Shit, I spent the $50,000 buyout already.

For this teacher the damage has been done. There is no going back. It is a major loss for the students, the parents, the school culture, and for the teacher and his family, a deep personal and professional loss. It's a process that promotes the loss of skilled teachers doing what they do best and a loss of the skills they possess that could be transferred to younger teachers.

My sense is that the problems associated with the loss of skilled teachers runs even deeper. It's about talented teachers being lured into thinking that what they do well should suddenly be ended, that somehow being bought out is the natural path and outcome to a successful career and should be done as soon as possible when teachers reach a certain point in their career, such as age fifty-five. It's the thing to do, even if one wants to stay.

There is great pressure to leave rather than stay because that way of thinking and behaving and making decisions is so much a part of our current school culture. Veteran teachers are offered a great many reasons to leave, such as less stress and the promise that life will be better, but they are offered few reasons to stay or assurances that they are needed. There currently exist few if any alternatives to these age-determined early-retirement buyouts.

Teachers need to be given the time to consider all sides of the process—both positive and negative—the value and necessity of their work versus walking out the door and never being able to come back; the exciting and hectic classroom in which many kids', parents', and even their own lives were changed in so many positive ways; the question of how they will spend their retirement time. It's not a decision to be rushed into.

The *New York Times* series *Room for Debate* considered the question, "Why Blame the Teachers?" and put the argument to retain our highly skilled veteran teachers into perspective. The following are comments from contributors to that series.

In his piece "Reform Driven by Education Fads,"[5] Pedro Noguera, executive director of the Metropolitan Center for Urban Education, suggests that an honest assessment of the tenure and teacher assignment rules in place in most school districts shows that change is needed. Removing incompetent teachers is too slow and arduous a process.

He says we need to find ways to reward teachers who consistently excel in providing support for their students and to retain highly skilled teachers in schools and classrooms that serve low-income children. None of the policy measures being considered address these challenges. In fact, they are likely to exacerbate problems if we create perverse incentives for school districts to lay off senior teachers, who are paid more, without an objective means of evaluating their effectiveness in the classroom.

Noguera says effective teaching requires a number of skills that typically cannot be acquired in one or two years or that can simply be measured by analyzing student test scores. This is the point that many of those leading the current wave of reform and the attacks on teachers don't understand. New

York Mayor Michael Bloomberg recently asserted that a person did not need experience in order to be an effective teacher.

For nearly ten years the Gates Foundation promoted the idea that creating small schools would lead to higher levels of student performance. After spending more than two billion dollars and obtaining mixed results, the foundation abandoned the initiative and replaced it with a set of initiatives designed to judge teachers by student test scores.

Noguera concludes that these examples illustrate much of what is wrong with the current direction of the education debate. He says we can't afford to let our schools to be disrupted by well-financed experiments or by politicians who want to use the current budget crisis to undermine the teaching profession. Recruiting and retaining effective teachers must remain central to all efforts to improve America's schools. But too often, those leading reform efforts have never taught nor spent much time observing effective teachers at work. Their lack of knowledge about teaching is a serious threat to creating the schools we need.

In her piece "What Politicians Don't Know,"[6] Molly Putnam, a seven-year teacher of government and economics at the High School of Telecommunications Arts and Technology in Brooklyn, says the most successful teachers are usually the most experienced ones. The majority of senior teachers are extremely effective educators who have strong classroom management skills and know best how students learn. Schools need these teachers to be mentors, leaders, coaches, and stabilizers. The most effective schools have the lowest teacher turnover rates.

Putnam says college graduates are not going to be attracted to a profession that only encourages short stints. The majority of teachers did not choose their profession because of vacation time or the salary or because they thought it would be easy. They chose teaching because they wanted to make a difference in children's lives. Those teachers who enter the profession for the more mundane reasons don't actually stay for very long.

Schools need to understand that to attract the best new teachers, they need to mentor them, give them proper resources and provide worthwhile professional development so they don't fail. And they need senior teachers to take the lead in those key roles.

Putnam suggests we imagine a large school system where students are taught almost entirely by recent college graduates who are earning a small salary to work for a couple of years before moving on to the "real" professions. It may be a politician's dream to alleviate the budget and pension crisis, but is this what is best for our children?

Noguera and Putnam provide a clear picture of the value of highly skilled teachers and why they are needed as mentors, leaders, coaches, and stabilizers. Theirs is a necessary argument for detouring and stopping the wave of buyouts of successful senior teachers that is causing a brain drain of our most talented teachers. The exodus leaves, as Putnam suggests, a school system where students are taught almost entirely by recent college graduates working for a couple of years before they move out an on to their "real" professions.

As the next chapter reveals, the concerns and fears of Noguera and Putnam are rapidly taking root in our schools. A strategy that can destroy our school systems is gaining strength, enveloping our students, parents, teachers, administrators, and school board members in an "every man for himself" environment. Everyone in the school community is reaching for a life jacket, but there are not enough to go around. Some will not make it if the current environment continues.

The most vulnerable, the students, will suffer as the new school year loses its beginning glow in September, seeing larger classes, courses eliminated, and new teachers who are unprepared for the real world of school. The novice and mid-career teachers will battle the veteran teachers to stay afloat and keep their jobs, pressing the most senior teachers to take a buyout, pack their bags, and "do the right thing" by making more jobs available for them.

In the worst case scenario teachers will face layoffs or firing if states such as Indiana, Wisconsin, Ohio, and New Jersey follow through on their proposals to end seniority and teacher tenure as a way to reduce budget shortfalls. Suddenly, in the spring of 2011, this unexpected element gains power in the already potent assaults headed toward our schools. The "out with the old, in with the new" approach may gain a powerful tool if the safe haven of tenure and seniority collapses.

We will be left, as Putnam suggests, with schools in which students are taught almost entirely by inexperienced college and alternative certification graduates along with a small cadre of mid-career teachers. They have survived so far, but will they know how to proceed in September as the new school year begins? Will the now destabilized school environment be the scene of increased discipline problems, low morale, poor student performance, dissatisfaction among parents, and more budget cuts? Will our large secondary schools see an increase in dropouts, crises, violence, and absenteeism among both students and staff?

I will address additional factors involved in the creation of this situation and the interventions needed to avert it. There is a massive brain drain of highly skilled teachers occurring, spurred on by a well-intended but ill-conceived strategy to offer high-salaried older teachers early buyouts so their salaries can be used to hire three novice teachers. I label this destructive process the three-for-one epidemic.

This situation is of our own making, leaving our most skilled, experienced and loyal veteran teachers no other career option than to retire, taking with them a legacy of successful teaching, wisdom, and classroom skills that could be used to mentor novice teachers as well as failing mid-career or veteran teachers.

We need to find ways to reverse this trend, thereby increasing retention and performance of the entire teaching staff and eliminating the turbulence now occurring in our schools. Schools with faculties of inexperienced teachers and few mid-career and veteran teachers to ask for help, and with overwhelmed administrators who are losing veteran teachers to retirement, are losing their most supportive allies, political advisors, and mentors. The current trend leaves in its wake no winners, only losers.

NOTES

1. William L. Fibkins, *An Administrator's Guide to Better Teacher Mentoring*, 2nd ed. (Lanham, MD: Rowman and Littlefield, 2011), 151.

2. Fibkins, *An Administrator's Guide to Better Teacher Mentoring*, 181.

3. Robert Butler, *Ageism in America*, Report of the Anti-Ageism Task Force (New York, NY: International Longevity Center, 2006), 19–21.

4. Butler, *Ageism in America*, 23.

5. Pedro Noguera, "Reform Driven by Education Fads," *New York Times*, March 6, 2011, http://nytimes.com/roomfordebate/2011/03/06/why-blame-the-teachers/reform-drive (accessed March 7, 2011).

6. Molly Putnam, "What Politicians Don't Know," *New York Times*, March 6, 2011, http://nytimes.com/roomfordebate/2011/03/06/why-blame-the-teachers/what-politicians-don't-know (accessed March 7, 2011).

Chapter 2

The Three-for-One Epidemic Is Causing the Brain Drain of Our Best Veteran Teachers

In the next decade about half of U.S. teachers will become eligible for retirement. As a result there is a nationwide effort taking place to encourage the most experienced and highest-paid teachers to retire early by offering a financial incentive known as a buyout. The buyout option is designed to avoid layoffs of current staff and to hire inexperienced novice teachers to replace the cadre of retiring older teachers, many of whom are highly successful and described as "irreplaceable." In the worst case scenario schools will simply not fill the positions being vacated in order to fund even more young recruits.[1]

I label this early retirement plan the "three-for-one" package. No, it's not a MacDonald's promotion where you get three burgers for the price of one. Rather, it's a plan to encourage experienced teachers to retire so the district can hire two or three novice teachers for the cost of the veteran teacher's salary and benefits. This early-retirement frenzy is not unexpected. Many school districts are facing serious fiscal problems, and getting rid of experienced teachers seems to be the favored option.

However, this option has taken on a negative tone in many districts. Financial desperation can bring out the worst, often self-serving behaviors, not only in families but in institutional life. Close relationships among school staff, built on trust and mutual support, can be strained or even destroyed when financial problems arise in tough economic times.

This kind of toxic atmosphere often produces a school culture in which young and mid-career teachers, leery of losing jobs, are pitted against veteran teachers who say they are not ready to retire. Survival, saving one's job, everyone for him- or herself, can become the norm, with the young and mid-career teachers advocating, sometimes very aggressively, for the older teachers to opt for retirement in order to provide them a safety net.

11

Ironically, these can be the same teachers who were mentored and supported as novices by the older teachers they are now trying to push out. Close professional bonds can die fast when one's livelihood seems at stake. This atmosphere can also pit the district administration against highly successful veteran teachers who want to remain in their classrooms and say they are not ready to retire.

For many of these star teachers, the classroom has been their second home and their life's blood. Asking them to throw their careers away for, as one teacher told me, a "bag of gold," doesn't sit well, given all they have contributed to the students, parents, colleagues, and community. As the same teacher said, "I feel like all the hard work I put in amounts to nothing. I thought I was a somebody—valued, important. What a fool! But I still have my pride in what I have accomplished here and I am not about to give it up so they can use my salary and benefits to hire a bunch of kids with no experience."

Saying "no" to a buyout is not easy for highly successful teachers who want to remain in their classrooms. A culture of young versus old, in which self-interest reigns, can ensue when getting rid of older teachers becomes *the* option to save the district from financial problems. The burden of solving the district's fiscal problems is placed on the backs of older teachers, many of whom have been highly successful and known for their dedication and skills among students, parents, colleagues, and community members. There is subtle and sometimes aggressive pressure put on them to take an early buyout, pack their bags, and leave.

The buyout option is often sold to older teachers by describing them as saviors who are giving up their teaching careers to save the district, heroes to the end of their careers. The decision to stay or go, often given with only a few months to decide, is not easy. The district administrators, school board, and most younger teachers want them out.

If they refuse and don't buy into the savior or hero role, then the labels assigned to their not going are often negative, hostile, and hurtful. In this atmosphere the highly successful star teacher can overnight become the problem teacher because he or she won't go. There is often pressure from veteran teachers who do opt to retire to go out as a group—"we came in together, worked together, have fond memories together, so let's leave as one."

This push for a fast exit often carries a subtle message for veteran teachers who choose to stay: "You will be vilified, made a scapegoat for the district's financial problems, seen as self-serving, and seen as causing the layoffs of colleagues. You will pay a price for saying no to our generous offer. And you could find yourself being moved to a different grade level or school where you will be isolated. Take the buyout and save yourself and your legacy."

What's missing for young and mid-career teachers in this assault on older teachers who refuse to retire is the awareness that some day they may be in a similar position when they reach retirement age. What goes around comes around. The aggressor becomes the victim, so be careful what you wish for. It may return to haunt you.

This is a no-win situation for all involved. Caring and honorable school administrators and school board members are forced into playing hardball with veteran teachers whom they have long looked to for leadership, counsel, and support. I say hardball because the fast-rising storm of budget problems is forcing them into taking drastic measures that go against their own sense of fair play and dignity. In these high-pressure situations time is a major factor, often leaving administrators and school board members little time or guidance to consider alternatives other than eliminating their veteran teacher corps through buyouts.

One alternative might be offering the best and brightest veteran teachers a reason and incentive to stay, in order to ensure a sense of stability for students, parents, novice teachers just coming on board, anxious mid-career teachers who face layoffs, and building principals who fear losing their most experienced, supportive and trusted allies. These buyouts can decimate the principals' leadership teams at a time when they are much needed to help guide the school though troubled times, not losing their skills to the buyout process.

This alternative can encourage teachers who have long wanted out of their classrooms to leave but sell skilled veteran teachers on the need to stay. It can also reduce the hostility and divisions that often arise in an environment where the security of staff members is threatened.

Here is a story, told to me by a high school math teacher, of what can happen when the three-for-one conditions take hold in a school and the fast exit of veteran teachers is the only solution.

It's as if they want me to do community service. Give up the job I love in order to make room for new teachers, kids, really, who have no idea what teaching here at the high school is really like. Hey, I don't deserve being placed in this no-win situation. If I stay I'll be maligned and the opposition will come at me in full force until they force me out. But if I go I'll be doing it against everything I believe in and have worked so hard to achieve. I love what I am doing and I'm still able to deliver what the kids need to succeed.

When I find myself not up to being the best, then I'll be the first one out of here. But I am not there yet and I am not going to let anyone push me out. I'll decide that on my own. If I allow this to happen to me, I'll be letting my students down. I tell my students to follow their dreams and not let anyone tell them they can't. I'm still following my dream and teaching is who I am, what I do, and I'm good at it.

You know, I never thought I'd see the day when all my hard work is being rewarded with a few bucks buyout and a "you better go" chorus from colleagues, administrators and some parents I once trusted. Now they are turning on me and other veteran teachers who are nearing retirement age. Some good-bye! You know what; I have done enough service to the community in the thirty years I've been here. This is not a problem of my making and I am not going to be a scapegoat for someone else's poor decision making. I hope I am strong enough to stand my ground.

I feel really bad for some of my friends who want to stay but are afraid to stand up and fight. They are going quietly and my sense is that they'll regret their decisions a few months into retirement. I hope God gives us vets the courage to say "no, I'm not going" and that we stick together as one and fight back, but I am not sure some of us are up to a fight.

As another teacher told me,

I can't believe they are doing this to us. Did everything we did to help kids even matter? I know [the principal] feels terrible but as principal he has no choice but to push us to take the buyout. He's got to follow the party line or his head will be on the chopping block along with ours. The way things are going, the Board of Ed will have to order a bigger chopping block, with all the teachers who will be packing their bags. By next year the school will be run by a bunch of new college grads. God help our students and those new teachers, too. They are going to need lots of help but there will be nobody here to answer their call.

The older teachers who choose to stay and continue their work are not the only ones facing hard choices. Building administrators, charged with encouraging older teachers to retire, also find themselves pitted against the district administration, school board, and even the young and mid-career teachers in their buildings. The district administration and school board plan the buyout but they are not the major enforcers. Nor are the young and mid-career teachers. They can mouth their feelings in the faculty room and engage in psychological warfare to make the older teachers feel unwanted but they are not the ones to pull the "you're out" cord.

Rather, it is the building administrator who is placed in a position to encourage highly successful veteran teachers to cut short their careers, often the same teachers who have been supportive, loyal, and instrumental in improving the school climate and who have served as a buffer to ward off political attacks by disgruntled staff, parents, and community members. These teachers are often allies, who have superior classroom and mentoring skills, have played leadership roles, have hard-earned experience in the trenches, have wisdom and are politically savvy.

Some of them have been part of their administrator's inner circle, serving as guide, mentor, advisor, and antenna to student, staff, parent, and community issues. They are a group tested by the battles of school life, who were able to sense where the right path lay to improve the school.

Building administrators are charged, like it or not, with the dirty work of getting these same trusted teachers to accept a buyout plan, whether the teachers like it or not. Administrators and star teachers are forced into roles that can rob each of their trust, dignity, and care for each other. It's a difficult role, especially for the administrator, knowing the hard truth that the buyout option could decimate the cadre of highly successful teacher leaders and make his or her job more difficult or even impossible. These administrators know the hard truth that y can't oppose or stymie the buyout program or they, too, might be asked to leave. Survival often wins out when one's job is on the line.

With no good choices, most administrators choose to go along while very aware that the fast exit of these successful teachers will present major setbacks for their programs and the school climate they have worked to create. This cadre of teachers can probably not be replaced in the near future, maybe ever. Experience counts, and wise building administrators know they can't succeed on their own. It's like a World Series–winning baseball team trading their experienced star players for a group of inexperienced, untested minor league players. When experience is absent, trouble can start. The brain drain caused by the early retirement option for veteran teachers often results in a leadership gap, discipline problems, decrease in staff and administrator morale, and a rudderless school climate.

The early buyout of teachers can become a major burden and headache for many district superintendents. They have to carry out the mandate of the school board to use early buyouts to reduce the school budget, and this easily becomes a crippling and divisive role that has no winners. Managing a plan to get rid of longtime colleagues and friends and replace them with inexperienced and untried novices feels like an act of betrayal and stupidity to many superintendents I have spoken to privately. They are very much aware of the damage that can occur with this three-for-one buyout.

Their public demeanor has to appear caring, but all about numbers. However, it is often a personal trauma. As one superintendent told me, "You do what is required, be a good soldier, but believe me, it's an ongoing hell. No wonder no one wants to be a superintendent any more. It's not worth the heartaches, sleepless nights, and seeing all that you've built up over the years go up in flames in a few short months."

A report on State Pension Systems and School District Early Retirement Incentives[2] gives us a glimpse of what can occur in an early buyout process. The report states that teachers develop close ties to one another over the duration of their professional careers. Therefore, we should not underestimate the power of group cohesion, both in delaying retirement and in deciding to "jump ship" together. A superintendent should not be shocked if almost the entire senior staff of a school marches into the office and announces, "We came in together and we are going out together." If a number of teachers decide late in the school year to retire, the school administrator's quiet summer can quickly be thrown into turmoil as he or she scrambles to find high-quality replacements.

For this reason school districts often set a limited window to use early retirement incentives. They also specify a minimum period of time that must elapse between a teacher's notification of intent to retire and the actual retirement date.

One of the most damning aspects of early retirement incentives identified in the report for superintendents and building administrators is that even when districts are prepared for teacher retirements it may be difficult to recruit trained, experienced teachers to replace those who are leaving. With increasing state and federal mandates, school districts, especially those in urban and poorly funded school districts, can have difficulty finding teachers in such areas as special education, bilingual education, physics, and mathematics.

This three-for-one process results in loss at many levels—a loss of trust, loss of camaraderie, loss of a "can do" philosophy among staff, students and parents, and a loss of the caring skills and will to heal the real personal and professional wounds created in the buyout process.

When star teachers leave their settings, they leave a huge vacuum. The school, minus its departed elders, loses experience, wisdom, mentoring and advising skills, service as big brothers and big sisters to novice teachers, and a sense of history regarding hard-won efforts to make the school a better place for all. All of this is sometimes gone within just a few months.

In some school districts the teaching positions are left unfilled. In September students and parents may ask, "Whatever happened to Mr. Klein? He was the best. I was looking forward to taking his advanced lit class. Not only is he gone but the advanced lit class is not even being offered. And my friends tell me that Ms. Sharkey, Mr. Monroe, and Coach Murray are also gone. What happened? Like overnight, some of the best teachers left."

In many school districts, then, urging experienced teachers to retire early, without giving them some career alternatives for remaining as a valued member of the school community, is not as positive and rewarding as it is described in the district's promotion to parents and taxpayers. It is not, as it is sometimes touted, "a win-win for everyone—retiring teachers, staff not facing layoffs—and the opportunity for infusion of new blood with the hiring of young teachers."

As I have observed in many school districts, beneath this hype lies the truth: it is often a hostile, negative, pressured process that results in the hiring of novice teachers, no matter how well-trained, who can't be expected to take over the role of veteran teachers. The hope of the self-promotion of early buyouts doesn't tell the real story of what the loss of talented teachers will mean for the district in the near and distant future. The process is shortsighted.

What is shortsighted in the buyout process is its "one-size-fits-all" approach. It may be a good idea to give poor and mediocre teachers a way out of a job they dislike and each day hate to show up for. However, what needs to be considered are practical options to retain highly successful teachers who make up the heart and soul of the school's team of teaching curriculum and leadership. Options might include offering alternatives such as part-time, full–time, or flexible positions as consultants, teacher trainers, or mentors, choices put in place to actively sell the schools' best and brightest elders on staying on board and helping to keep the ship afloat.

Instead of a three-for-one option, let's move toward a one-for-one option. For example, if a star teacher decides to stay as a part-time mentor, at least one novice could be hired full time.

Getting star elder teachers to retire is a tragic waste of resources that can never be replaced, particularly if the buyout option is repeated and repeated, creating a culture that tells teachers that when they reach a certain age, their careers are over. That is no way to insure stability and continuity. There are other choices that must be considered. Our elder teachers have earned the right to choose whether to stay or go, in an unhurried, thoughtful, and supported manner, and be given options to continue their important work if they choose to stay.

Let's be creative in finding ways to retain our most precious resources, our star elder teachers, and not get caught up in shortsighted buyout options that leave our schools leaderless and manned by inexperienced staff. Let's value our elder staff and not place them in positions where they have to give up rewarding careers in order to supposedly "save" their school districts. The problem is not their fault, not a result of their actions. Why place the blame on them and in the process cause divisions among school staff and leave students without valued teachers?

There is currently great alarm in our school and communities about bullying of students, aggressive behavior in which some students identify one or a group of peers to pick on, isolate, push around, hurt, frighten, or make feel unwanted, unprotected, different, or otherwise targeted. The early buyout of elder teachers can result in "bullying" and pressure from peers and district administrators. If elder teachers choose to stay they may become the target of negative comments, destructive gossip, and innuendoes. When our professional or personal safety seems threatened, we can all become bullies, even teachers and administrators who instruct students in how to stop bullying in their schools. We are all human, and in the quest for survival, we are capable of unseemly, uncaring, destructive behavior.

If the one-size-fits-all buyout process continues, there will be serious ramifications with the exiting of highly successful veteran teachers, with serious impact on the entire school community and community at large. Veteran teachers at the top of their teaching game will take with them their hard-earned experience, skills honed over a lifetime of teaching, knowledge of their school and community, and a sense of what works for students and staff. Their exit en masse will surely bring about turmoil for students, remaining staff, and administrators who have long counted on their support and guidance but now find themselves with a leadership vacuum and only a few trusted allies to give them necessary feedback and direction.

Schools will become like poor-market baseball teams who have a yearly practice of trading their best players to wealthier teams, like the New York Yankees, in return for the necessary cash to stay financially stable, never getting to the playoffs or the World Series and remaining merely a farm club useful for developing players for the star teams. Those teams have no hopes or aspirations of being number one or two, instead settling for last or close to it. Such will be our schools if the buyouts of our talented vets continue.

Mediocrity will become a way of life as students are faced with ill-prepared teachers, a revolving door of new teachers, poor morale among an ever-changing faculty, administrators without teacher leaders to help address pressing school problems, and parents and community members who maybe once praised buyouts but find themselves questioning what went wrong when a number of veteran teachers suddenly retire.

In June they were in the classroom but by September they are gone. Their rooms are now inhabited by, as one teacher commented, "clueless kids just out of college who will be eaten alive by some of these students," or stand empty because courses taught by exiting teachers have been cut from the curriculum. Another masterful money saver—get a skilled veteran teacher to retire, hire two new teachers, and then eliminate the courses the veteran taught and put the money into the district fund. I label this an epidemic of "two for one and one for me," even more disturbing than the "three-for-one" approach in which three new teachers are hired. With "two for one and one for me," the students and parents get even more turmoil—fewer teachers and a loss of courses.

Either way, students, parents, staff, and building administrators lose, and it all seems to happen almost overnight. When students return to school in September they find a changed scene and rightfully ask questions.

What happened to Mrs. Cary? I was supposed to have her for advanced lit. I spoke to her last May about taking the course and she never said anything about leaving. Is she OK? Where did she go? She was too young and vibrant to retire, wasn't she? And I just heard the advanced lit course is no longer being offered. I was planning on taking it because I love lit and thought it would help me for early admission to college.

And I notice that Mr. Harrison, Ms. Thompson, and my soccer coach, Ms. Reynolds, aren't around. Did they leave, too? I also heard there's no more junior varsity soccer for girls. What happened to my school? And who are all these new teachers? They look so young. They can't be much older than me. I am pissed. I don't need this to happen in my senior year.

There are no winners in this scenario except low-performing and disgruntled veteran teachers who want out of the classroom as quickly as possible. Yes, there is a subtle effort on the part of some education leaders to smooth over the dire consequences that can come with the buyout of our best teachers. Here is an example.

Kerry Birmingham, Public Information Officer for the Michigan Education Association (MEA), suggests voluntary termination programs, sometimes known as retirement incentives, are increasingly popular. "We are seeing more and more of it," she says. "It's been a trend on and off for several years as school districts try to balance their budget and also maintain staff. There is often financial incentive for the retiring teachers as well as the school district because they are most likely to bring in younger teachers, or in some cases not replace the retiring teachers."[3]

Birmingham also suggests that unlike other budget-cutting measures like four-day school weeks, termination of retirement-eligible veteran teachers doesn't present concern for student learning. She says, "It doesn't necessarily have a negative impact because the teachers that are coming in are trained teachers. However, one concern is that these new faculty members will be inexperienced. We still need to make sure that we have mentor teachers for the youngest teachers coming in. We don't want, in any school districts, a staff of all brand-new teachers."

All this sounds not too troubling until one focuses on the concerns found in Ms. Birmingham's words. Concerns abound. For example:

- "most likely to bring in younger teachers"
- "in some cases not replace the retiring teachers"

- "doesn't necessarily have a negative impact because the teachers coming in are trained teachers"
- "these new faculty members will be inexperienced"
- "need to make sure that we have mentor teachers for the youngest teachers"
- "we don't want, in any school districts, a staff of brand-new teachers"

This remedy for school districts' financial problems is filled with time bombs that can and will explode throughout the school community once in place. Getting rid of our best and brightest veteran teachers will leave an experience vacuum. Then they bring in young, inexperienced teachers and are foolish enough to think it will not have a negative impact on student learning. Then they get around to being concerned about the lack of experience on the part of these newly arrived novices as they struggle to survive. Finally, when it is too late, they suggest we need experienced teacher mentors to come to the aid of the newcomers. When they discover that most of the experienced veterans, who had the right stuff to mentor the newcomers, have taken the buyouts and time bombs are exploding across the school landscapes, the school districts quickly learn the crisis that they created, almost overnight, a faculty dominated by young, inexperienced teachers who are themselves at risk of failure.

A faculty composed of newcomers who themselves need mentoring are now the power players of the school. In a mental hospital parallel, the patients have taken over the asylum! Concerns? You bet! The education leaders who have planned this so-called wise intervention are back in their safe offices as these bombs explode in October. The quiet days of September, filled with new beginnings, hopes, and dreams of what might be are quickly being replaced in October with the political push and shove that is sure to surface.

Students will have more behavior and discipline problems, faculty morale will decrease as the poorly skilled staff look for support and mentoring that is no longer available, staff attendance will suffer, parents will demand changes, and building administrators will be targeted for ineffective leadership because they lack the veteran staff to address the ongoing crisis. It's the kids, parents, skeleton crew of experienced teachers who are left ,and building administrators who must put out the fires, fires that would not have started if the highly skilled veteran teachers were sold on staying on board.

However, the problems faced by skilled veteran teachers go beyond choosing early retirement packages. Times have changed. The age at which people used to retire, generally 55 to 65, has changed. Many people eligible for retirement at ages 55 to 65 want to continue to stay in the workforce and work at their current or related positions on either a full-time or part-time basis.

They look to their employers to offer flexible positions so they can continue to contribute. They are not interested in packing their bags and heading off into the supposed calm of retirement life. They want to remain in the action.

No, not every aging worker has the interest, dedication, or desire to remain on board. Those who disliked, even hated, their jobs are looking for a buyout. But for successful veteran employees the story is different. They've enjoyed life as a successful employee. Yes, there have been bumps and failures, but they've weathered the storm and are at the top of their game. The same is true for successful veteran teachers. We dishonor them by proposing a buyout instead of telling them we need them to stay, that we will work with them to keep them on either a full-time or part-time basis.

These are the men and women we look to in order to keep our schools humming and running right. We have to say to them, "We need you. We're flexible. Work with us. This is not about retiring but about staying and helping us navigate through the tough situation we are in."

There are better ways to survive as caring institutions and communities, even when our school districts are facing a dire fiscal environment. What appears to be a well-intentioned effort to save jobs through early buyouts of veteran teachers can have unintended negative consequences. Let's visit the world of early retirement for the highest-paid and most experienced workers. What is the message they are hearing?

NOTES

1. Thomas G. Carroll and Elizabeth Foster, *Who Will Teach? Experience Matters* (Washington, DC: Commission on Teaching and America's Future, 2010), 1–3, http://nctaf.org/WhoWillTeach?ExperienceMatters.htm (accessed October 17, 2010)

2. Frank V. Auriemma, Bruce S. Cooper, and Stuart C. Smith, *Graying Teachers: A Report on State Pension Systems and School District Early Retirement Incentives* (Eugene, OR: ERIC Clearinghouse on Educational Management, 1992), 22, 23, 75.

3. Brandon Howell, "Schools Offer Early Retirement Incentive," *Capital News Service*, April 16, 2010, http://capitalnewsservice.wordpress.com/2010/04/16/schools-offer-early-retirement-incentive (accessed November 10, 2010).

Chapter 3

Veteran Teachers Are Joining the Ranks of Skilled Workers Being Bought Out in Every Sector of the Economy

The early buyouts and layoffs of veteran workers go far beyond the school house. It is happening in almost every public and private sector in America. It is causing not only a brain drain of our most experienced workers but often is leading to their being replaced with part-time workers, temporary workers, independent consultants, and freelance workers. Or, in many cases, simply not replacing them at all.

Marc Freedman of Encore and Civic Ventures, a think tank for boomers, work and social purpose, reports that "millions of U.S. workers in their fifties and sixties have been downsized, outsourced, replaced by offshore workers, bought out, eased out, or laid off. Many professions, from law to journalism, appear to have adopted their own versions of the navy's 'thirty years and out, at least for those who don't make admiral.'"[1]

This dark picture of the brain drain occurring in the public and private workforce does have many helpful lessons for school board members, administrators, and pro-education parent and community proponents as they face budget cuts in their schools, that is if they can listen, given the pressure they are under to cut senior staff. Buyouts and hiring of new workers are not without cost and not without implications for performance.

These are important lessons because the public schools are seeing the beginning of such a staffing model. For example, in one large urban district buyouts have decimated the school psychologist staff. Two of the three psychologists have accepted a buyout and retired. The remaining psychologist, who served one large urban high school of 1,500 students before the buyouts is now force to add two other large junior high schools with enrollments of over 1,200 students each to his workload. He is now required to work part-time in three different settings with a total enrollment of 3,900 students.

23

It is an impossible task for him. Not only is he unable to address the mental health needs of so many students and parents, but also he has no time to establish roots in each school and, get to know and offer support to the faculty and administration. Moreover he is likely to be unavailable when a crisis hits because he will be off in another building.

When the students return to school in September not only will they find some familiar faces missing, they will also find a major source of mental health support missing from their daily school life. When buyouts and layoffs happen, things change for both the school and workplace environments, often for the worse.

Rob Silverblatt writes that buyouts lure 9,000 state workers into retirement.[2] Looking to shield their workforces from tumultuous cutbacks, at least six cash-strapped states—Connecticut, Maine, New York, Oklahoma, Louisiana, and Vermont—have decided to spend millions on incentives to encourage government employees to retire. Silverblatt says there is a concern that the buyouts can lead to a brain drain if too many experienced employees accept. Connecticut lost 12 of its 23 prison wardens, 200 state college professors, and 10 percent of its teachers at technical high schools in its recent round of buyouts. All told, 3,856 employees in Connecticut have accepted the offer.

Connecticut State Representative Christopher Caruso (D) described one downside of the buyout process: "What ends up happening is the incentives are very, very attractive, so many people who have institutional history with state agencies opt to take early retirement. So we frankly drain those agencies of institutional histories of experience."

Silverblatt adds that at least sixteen states were forcing upward of 593,000 employees to take unpaid furloughs in 2010. Meanwhile, at least 54,000 state workers, including teachers, have been laid off.

The buyout incentives have a history of not always delivering projected cost savings. Silverblatt says if states too quickly refill the jobs opened by the buyouts, they have to absorb the cost of the incentive while still paying salaries to new workers. To salvage its savings from buyouts, Maine's legislature has required that all except critical positions be kept empty for two years. In a 2003 experiment with buyouts in Connecticut, 983 workers were rehired under temporary contracts and were paid around fourteen million dollars in salaries in addition to their pensions.

In 2009, 1,521 workers in Tennessee accepted buyouts, but only employees holding "expendable" posts were eligible to step down so that those jobs could be left permanently vacant. In New York officials are currently vetting positions to see which could be left open after retirements. Only workers in those jobs deemed "dispensable" will be able to accept the incentive.

Management consultant Nancy Dering Martin told Silverblatt, "Overall, even if retirees' jobs are filled by new workers who earn less money, state agencies could lose thousands of dollars per hire in training and lost productivity. Rehiring is not without cost; it's not without implications for performance."

Numbers like 9,000; 3,856; 593,000; and 1,521 don't mean much by themselves. But they take on great meaning when we are talking about real people, workers and their families whose lives may be upended, some damaged and some changed forever by taking retirement buyouts that they soon regret.

As Representative Caruso says, when they leave they drain those agencies of institutional histories of experience. They leave the remaining agency staffs overworked if the positions are not filled with newcomers. And if they are replaced, staffs are saddled with training and caring for these inexperienced newcomers who don't even know where the bathrooms are or where to get a burger for lunch, never mind the more serious issues of learning their jobs, the politics of the place, whom to trust and whom to keep at arm's length. Problems arise for both the newcomers and the remaining experienced staff.

Here is what happens in those agencies or businesses when staff are not replaced or newcomers come on board:

- Customers, clients, and interested/concerned citizens' phone calls and e-mails don't get returned.
- The phones are busy, busy, busy and callers can't get through to a person.
- There is a long wait for help, either on the phone, by e-mail, or in person. The message says, "Please understand that we are understaffed due to budget cuts. We are doing the best we can."
- If a caller asks for a specific person, for example, Ms. Nelson, the response might be, "Ms. Nelson is no longer with us. She took early retirement." Or even worse, "Ms. Nelson was laid off and she is not being replaced."
- There is a high rate of absenteeism among older workers who want out and newcomers who are struggling to figure out the job. Or, both groups call in sick because they are looking for new jobs.
- There is an increase in political cronyism to retain "people like us who came up the hard way." These people somehow survive the "dispensable" or "expendable" list.

The depleted staff is faced not only with the loss of key coworkers but also the boss, such as the prison wardens in Connecticut. Increasingly the bosses are replaced by a series of temps, not full-time employees, often political hacks or failed CEOs, who are not committed to these temporary positions.

Wall Street Journal reporter Joe Light sheds a new light on this growing process in his article, "When the New Temp Happens to be the Boss."[3] Light says companies have used temporary administrative assistants and customer service representatives for years. But soon, more employees may find temps in the unlikely position of being the boss. In some cases companies are looking for people to shepherd reorganizations, layoffs, or other transitions. Light quotes Lorrie Lykins, director of research services for the Institute for Corporate Productivity, who says, "It can be less painful to have a contingent manager to do that." Lykins adds, "In the coming years, we're going to see a sea change in who the typical contingent worker is."

Light also says having temps in higher-level roles can affect the attitudes of the permanent employees they work alongside. He quotes Joseph Broschak, management professor at the University of Arizona, who said, "Full-time employees wonder what it means and if they're valued less because temps have replaced some of them." Replacing a manager with a temporary employee could make his or her reports question the long-term viability of their department.[4]

This is the kind of process that can and will happen in our schools if the buyouts and layoffs continue—permanent teaching jobs eliminated by buyouts and layoffs and replaced by a revolving door of temporary substitutes, and administrative jobs eliminated by buyouts and layoffs, replaced by temporary former administrators who have no roots or experience in the community. These changes can create a leaderless, "who's in charge?" school climate in which ownership, responsibility, and caring can quickly disappear.

The job market is grim for older workers in the private and public sectors, such as teachers and administrators who have taken a buyout or have been laid off but want to return to work. *Newsday*'s Mark Miller reports that laid-off workers face multiple obstacles. He reports that while older workers are less likely to be laid off, they are facing a much harder time finding new work than younger seekers. Researchers from the Urban Institute say workers aged fifty-one to sixty-one who have lost their jobs are one-third less likely to find new work than their counterparts aged twenty-five to thirty-four. Workers over sixty-two were half as likely to be reemployed.

Johnson also touches on the ageism issue, citing that age discrimination claims filed with the Equal Opportunity Commission have spiked in recent years. Richard Johnson says, "Employers are clearly reluctant to hire older workers. Many are concerned that older workers are more expensive than younger ones. That they lack up-to-date skills, that they won't be around long enough to justify the cost of hiring and training them. These concerns are mostly unfounded, but they're widespread. If that's not outright age discrimination, it certainly comes close."[5]

Being old, wanting to work, but not finding work can be upsetting. The *Sloan Center News* article, "Older Adults Struggle in Job Search," reports that while some older workers may need, and want, to have jobs, their plans may not be realized. Losing one's job and not finding another can bring about serious physical and emotional problems.

Jacquelyn James, research director for the Sloan Center for Aging and Work, says, "Being summarily dismissed from the workplace can really be damaging to the self-esteem of older adults. Feelings of embarrassment can also make it difficult to reach out to networks and friends. And such stress and anxiety can further hinder an older job seeker's prospects, even their desire to actively search for a job." The Sloan report says a large majority of older workers reported symptoms of stress, such as uneasiness and restlessness, strain in family relations, change in sleeping patterns, and avoidance of social situations.[6]

This data is important for senior teachers who may be too hasty or rushed when considering a retirement buyout. The data suggests that if you retire and then regret your decision and want to return to teaching or explore a new career, the jobs may not be there. Retiring can have a negative cost in one's physical and emotional condition as well as in family and social life. Therefore, it seems to be prudent for both teacher unions and school boards to provide in-depth counseling as part of the buyout process, preferably offered by former teachers and administrators who have already retired and know both the upside and downside of the retirement scene.

Here is a short vignette I wrote that will help focus on the experience that a retired teacher or administrator can offer a potential buyout candidate. This vignette, "Why Am I Looking for Work When I Don't Have To?" is included in my unpublished manuscript, "The Dark and Sometimes Humorous Side of Retirement and Aging."[7]

I've got this monkey on my back, kind of a demon that preys on me every day. It's a feeling that I have to get a job, and soon. It's weird feeling this way because I don't need a job. I'm not rich but I have more than enough to live on. Enough money to go to Florida for three months each winter. I've been to the Caribbean, Europe, and Australia. And I belong to two golf clubs, one here in New York and the other in Florida. Still, I'm not happy. Something is missing and I think it's a job.

You see, a job would give me a set schedule. The people at my job would expect me to show up, be accountable, and I'd be missed if not there. With a job I could meet people, be part of a team, be recognized and needed as a contributor. That's something I've had all my working life, until I retired. I've got time on my hands. It's so hard to while away my time vacuuming the carpet, cleaning the toilets, washing the windows, cutting the lawn, doing the laundry and checking my e-mail and phone messages. I get out of the house by going to the post office, shopping, working out at the gym and playing golf. But it's not enough. I'm still left with too much idle time.

It drives me crazy. I find myself falling into the habit of being an observer. I'm watching life go by rather than being part of it. I'm on the bench instead of in the ball game, observing what goes on around me. Like the cops hanging out and drinking coffee while truckers speed by at eighty miles an hour in a thirty-five-mile-an-hour zone. Like the town workers sitting in their trucks doing nothing. The teenagers skipping school. Homeless people begging for money. Kids vandalizing the local parks. The lady next door having an affair with the plumber as soon as her husband leaves for work—must have a lot of plumbing problems in that house!

In observing my world I see more than I want or need to. When I had a full-time job I saw none of this "I don't care" behavior. And you know what? I was better off. I've become the observer, not the producer. In my work I traveled all over the country and met many interesting people. But when I retired my world became infinitely smaller. I drive the same three or four roads every day, and going to Florida is really only an escape. All I do is play golf, sit around drinking after the games, go to early-bird dinners getting drunk and talking about who died.

And that's true for many of my friends. They, too, have been transformed into observers. And like me they find themselves thinking about getting job in order to be contributors, not just retirees. However, the reality is that we are all overqualified and too old. Yes, we see ads in the papers and send out resumes, but no one calls us.

I even went to a job counselor at the state employment agency for help. Guess what he told me. "Take your age and some of your skills and experiences off the resume. Hey, you're more qualified than I am. You could take my job. Have you thought about volunteering?"

In a way it's a double whammy. The feeling that I need a job haunts me but when I search for a job, no one seems to notice me or value my experience. No one calls back. Maybe I need to learn how to stop looking for a job to solve my loneliness but if I stop thinking about and looking for a job, I'll have even more time on my hands. What will take its place?

Surely I don't need to drink more and sit around sunny Florida. I'll be dead in a few years if I keep that up. But volunteering? I don't want to be one of those old guys manning the information center and coffee shop at the local hospital. Jesus, has it come to this?

Retirement can have its cost, as seen in this vignette, if it leads to losing one's "place." That includes a place to show up each morning, perform the work you like doing and get paid for it, socialize with colleagues, celebrate good times like family achievements, birthdays, or anniversaries, grieve with each other over bad news, and honor colleagues who leave the workplace due to retirement or layoffs.

The data also suggests that there is an appearance of age discrimination by some employers in hiring older workers. But what Miller doesn't say is that age discrimination may be a subtle but important reason in buying out highly skilled veteran teachers. As I pointed out in chapter 1, schools are largely settings for the young—students, parents, and young novice teachers, who bring with them energy, enthusiasm, and spirit. Older staff can and do get stereotyped in this youth culture, particularly if they are not aging well and show some signs of slowing down. They may still be great teachers, desiring to stay in the classroom, but find themselves suddenly viewed as "old timers" and teachers who "won't be around long enough to justify their high salaries."

In my experience as an education reformer, I see ageism alive and well in our schools. Ageism often exists quietly below the surface but can be a potent force in the fast exiting of veteran teachers through buyouts, a force that can help convince them that they should pack their bags even though they continue to perform at a high level. I call it the "guess I'm getting too old" syndrome.

It's often not an intentional or planned assault. However, when budget cuts arise and buyouts are proposed for veteran teachers, ageism can become a powerful weapon, used by groups of otherwise honorable and caring novice and mid-career staff to aggressively persuade veterans to leave.

At its worst it is a manipulative tactic designed to make older teachers feel over the hill and consider a different lifestyle choice even though the one they have is working well for them and they are good at what they do. In politics it's a tactic that emphasizes all the reasons to retire and few if any to stay.

Older teachers hear comments such as, "If I were you I'd grab the buyout. Didn't you hear the rumors that the ninth graders coming from the junior high are terrors? Why stay and deal with those hell raisers? And what happens to you if they abolish tenure and seniority? You'll be out with nothing but your pension. I hear Medicare payments are going up and services are being reduced. What happens to your mom and dad on Medicare? That's going up, too. Be wise. Run for your life. It may be your last chance. Take the golden parachute and fly. Why stay here and work your butt off?

When they hear this theme becoming a loud chorus, growing louder by the day, even the most strong-of-heart teachers who want to stay in their classrooms can find their resolve being weakened. In the political world it's a tactic labeled "being played." One is moved by others' encouragement into supporting a position that goes against one's own self-interest. It's often a subtle sell. You don't see it coming or happening until you've signed on, and a short time later you are wondering why you did it.

It's a tactic sometimes employed by younger colleagues in schools, usually people of high moral standards and virtues, who are running scared, looking for ways to save their own jobs. Even the best of us can cross the line of decency when our jobs are on the line. Survivors often need big claws to hang on. It's psychological warfare aimed at steering older colleagues away from their hard-earned roles in the school hierarchy and away from their own best interest. It can be an all-too-easy process for those with the intent of getting their older colleagues to retire. They may not even be consciously aware of this intent, as they are acting out their own defense and survival mechanism, particularly when there is a battle on for scarce jobs in their schools.

Kids are not the only at-risk and vulnerable group in the school. Older teachers are also at risk and vulnerable as they suddenly find themselves in new and dangerous territory, at the fringe of the school community, isolated by the mounting group pressure on them to take a buyout as the acceptance or rejection date nears. This unaccustomed isolation can drive out the best and brightest of our older teachers. There are no winners in this scenario; novice, mid-career and veteran teachers are all being squeezed. When people are backed into a corner, it can bring out the worst behaviors in everyone concerned.

It's possible that veteran teachers will join the growing list of older workers filing claims of age discrimination with the Equal Opportunity Commission, particularly if tenure and seniority are eliminated.[8] Laying off or aggressively selling buyouts to older teachers may just rise to the level of age discrimination as seniority battles loom in a growing number of states, such as New York, Wisconsin, Indiana, Ohio, Florida, and New Jersey. It's something school boards, unions, administrators, and younger teachers need to think about.

Ken Dychtwald and colleagues in their book *Workforce Crisis* make clear the major arguments I am making in this book—that we need to create new leadership and mentoring roles for our highly skilled veteran teachers, giving them a reason and incentive to remain in their schools and help novice teachers become successful, even great, teachers and provide stability in these chaotic times. We must redefine the current role of veteran teachers as expendables who need to retire in order to make room for younger, inexperienced and less expensive novices. Dychtwald et al. say, "To expand the contributions of experienced workers, ask them to serve as trainers, coaches and mentors instead of hiring as many outside consultants."[9]

While they are not talking specifically about teachers as mature workers, their argument that older employees are our biggest untapped resource is central to our discussion. As they say, "companies already know how to shed mature workers through early retirement programs. But they don't know how to recruit or retain them." This is wrong for two reasons:

> Companies will need mature workers soon enough, well before the end of this decade in most industries in most developed countries. As workforce growth

slows and economic conditions improve, older workers as well as the already retired will become s source of skilled labor. In . . . health care, it's already here.

A company cannot develop a reputation that will attract the most talented
mature workers overnight. [It] must adjust the policies and practices of hiring
and retiring, and [it] must cultivate an environment that clearly welcomes and
values mature workers.[10]

Dychtwald et al. address the current upheaval in the workforce, suggesting
that

> we face an impending shortage of workers and skills, not a surplus, and so we
> must adjust to an ongoing condition of shortage. . . . Employers must now retain
> the services of skilled older workers rather than discharge them with pensions to
> make room for younger workers. . . . Given the increasing longevity, declining
> birthrates and disproportionate size of the baby boom generation now approach-
> ing traditional retirement age, we must look at the workforce quite differently
> and adapt our workforce management practices accordingly.[11]

Organizations and their leaders are going to need to make the most of their
talent supply today and ensure their talent supply tomorrow, despite ongoing
and impending changes in workforce composition.

Dychtwald and colleagues' research provides important data for their argument. Here are some examples:

- "The average age of employees will continue to rise and the workforce will
  become multigenerational. Proportionately, mature workers are the fastest-
  growing age segment, and large employers can expect to double their
  percentage of workers over fifty-five during the next five to ten years."
- "People are no longer 'acting their age.' Their life plans are no longer
  linear and predictable. They differ widely in how they integrate work and
  other pursuits into their lives."
- "Some CEO's make human resources a top priority but most don't."
- "As the baby boom generation reaches retirement age, organizations face
  a potentially debilitating brain drain of skills and experience."
- "Employers must not only require employees' continuing education but
  must provide that education directly to maintain needed skills."
- The whole range of management practices— compensation, benefits, and
  especially work arrangements—must appeal to the new workforce and accommodate the expanding variety of workers' needs and preferences."
- "As the workforce diversifies and disperses—adopting flexible sched-
  ules, telework and other technology-enabled arrangements—leaders
  must find new ways to cultivate and nourish organizational culture and
  identity."

- Diminished abilities of mature workers do not lead to low productivity. "With their extensive knowledge and experience, mature workers can compensate. . . . They simply work 'smarter.'"
- Early retirees report more health problems than do workers of the same age. . . . People who stay on the job . . . remain healthier and live longer. They enjoy the psychological benefits of contribution and self-esteem and the social benefits of a workplace community and its intergenerational exchange. . . . The best way to preserve one's brain power is to use it."
- The strengths of mature workers include "experience, emotional maturity and loyalty. . . . They practice teamwork and believe in service to others. Most prefer long-term connections with their employers and they associate their career with the company—not 'I'm in sales' but 'I'm an IBM salesman.'"
- "Mature workers report fewer issues with finances or indebtedness, marriage or relationships and parenting" than other cohorts.
- Mature workers "have the highest overall satisfaction with their jobs . . . and managers. They are most likely to say their pride comes from their work and career . . . and least likely to say they have too much work on their plates. . . . They are also least likely to say they feeling burnout, experiencing conflicts with colleagues, or in dead-end jobs. . . . They are most likely to report that the employer offers a congenial and fun workplace where teamwork rules and opportunities abound."
- Mature workers "have the highest percentage of any age group of people who really care about the fate of their organization and will spend extra effort to enable it to succeed."
- "Workers fifty-five and older want most to continue working past retirement age. Those sixty-five and older have the highest desire to keep working. Those who do intend to 'retire' from their employers plan to do so . . . at age sixty-six, on average—and 80 percent of them aim to work in retirement, most often part-time or in periods of working and not working."
- Mature workers want ten basic elements from employers. "Not surprisingly, a comprehensive retirement package tops the list, followed by a comprehensive benefits package (with emphasis on health coverage). The next several items entail work experience. Matures value the conditions for personal contributions, enjoyment and growth more highly than work arrangements (flexible schedule and location), and more than significant increases in compensation and vacation."[12]

Dychtwald and colleagues' assessment of the need to retain mature workers has an eerie quality to it. It's as if he is talking directly, in person, to school district and union leaders, urging them to give veteran teachers their hard-earned opportunity to provide leadership and mentoring, qualities now in high demand in our schools. Their time has come. They are needed in the great period of transition facing our schools. Some, not all, are ready for the challenge.

Here is their advice on what we should remember about mature workers:

> First, matures want to contribute meaningfully, potentially assuming leadership positions relatively late in their careers and bridging leadership gaps during organizational transitions. Do not overlook the leadership potential of "late bloomers."
>
> Second, . . . matures want to continue improving their skills and stretching their talents, but companies continually overlook them for training or development, with retirement on the horizon. Big mistake . . . since turnover tends to be lowest among older employees. . . . [And here is the main argument I am making in this book]*To expand the contributions of these experience workers, ask them to serve as trainers, coaches and mentors instead of hiring as many outside consultants* [emphasis added].
>
> Third, flexible work arrangements, especially flexible schedules, will matter increasing more as the proportion of mature workers increases. Flexibility must be a part of the employment deal, both as workers phase into retirement and as retirees return to work.[13]

Hopefully school district and union leaders will listen to this advice. However, the paradigm these authors present is in sharp contrast to the staffing model employed in our public schools. Our current model seems to emphasize hiring and retaining novice teachers, not retaining and utilizing the experience of highly skilled veteran teachers. It's as if the model Dychtwald and colleagues are proposing is turned upside down by leaders in the schools.

The current staffing model in the public schools is more in line with their observation that companies "know how to shed mature workers through early retirement programs."The prevalent attitude toward mature workers in the public schools is "out with the old, in with the new." As a result, the vast experience of many highly skilled veteran teachers is being driven to the margins of the school community, isolated and uninvited to join the school's future. Their dance card is empty.

I believe this is not an intentional abandonment of the resources of veteran teachers but simply the staff model that has been used over time, the "go-to" model when budget cuts are called form. It's the model school districts know, for good or bad. However, school districts need to make use of the talent supply they have today and ensure that it is there tomorrow by retaining the services of skilled older workers rather than discharging them with pensions to make room for younger workers.

School districts and union leaders need to change their staffing model to a new emphasis on retaining veteran teachers so they can train, coach, and mentor novices and serve as a stabilizing force, thus elevating human resources to a top priority. This process can grow talent at every level of the teaching staff, thrusting senior teachers into leadership roles and giving them the freedom to work rather than the freedom not to work that comes with being bought out.

In their book *The Support Economy*[14] authors and researchers Shoshona Zuboff and James Maxmin remind us why organizational changes such as buyouts of skilled veteran teachers are not the answer to school districts' staffing problems. They quote John Maynard Keyes' preface to *The General Theory of Employment, Interest and Money*:

> The composition of this book has been for the author a long struggle of escape, and so must the reading of it be for most readers if the author's assault upon them is to be successful, a struggle of escape from habitual modes of thought and expression. The difficulty lies not in the new ideas but in escaping from the old ones, which ramify, for those brought up, as most of us have been, into every corner of our minds.

Zuboff and Maxmin say "managers are seeking solutions, using management tools, old and new, available to them. They try everything in the kit from amputation to bolting on a new appendage. . . . They merge, they downsize . . . and it's OK, unless there is a bona fide discontinuity. At those times shoring up, paring down, adding on—not of it makes enough difference."

The following are some of Zuboff and Maxmin's observations on how organizations can forge a new model to supersede antiquated institutional barriers and self-protective mentalities. Clearly they apply to the current model used by school districts.

- "Organizations are like all living systems. . . . Every living system has its own unique 'deep structure,' a highly durable order that expresses its internal organization as well as the basic activities that define its existence and governs its interactions with the environment."
- "Occasionally . . . the system experiences a wholesale transformation of its deep structure, which must be disassembled in order for any fundamental changes to be accomplished."
- However, "like other living systems, . . . [it] is organized to reproduce itself at all costs, even when it is commercially irrational to do so. It is through these processes . . . that organizations defy change, even when they say they are changing."
- Such solutions as downsizing and streamlining to improve operational excellence and lower costs are "fragmented reflection[s] of the historical

forces engulfing us. Each is an effort to adapt these new forces at the margins of the organization, without disturbing its deep structure."

- "Typically people in organizations do not see what's coming. Events are not read as an indication that people should change what they are doing or how they are thinking. On the contrary, challenging events are often regarded as a signal that people should do the same thing they already know how to do, only even more assiduously than before. Sometimes these responses to grave challenges are deeply unhealthy and actually weaken the person, group or system, but people feel compelled to reproduce what they already know."

- However, "at the dawn of the twenty-first century, people have new dreams. . . . Today's people experience themselves first as individuals" and long for "psychological determination. . . . As a result of these new dreams a chasm has opened up between people and the organizations upon which they depend. People have undergone a discontinuity in mentality but organizations have not. . . . Individuals reach out from the intricacy of their lives in search of understanding, accommodation, and support, but the complexity of their needs and desire is ignored."

- People have changed more than the organizations upon which their well-being depends. Today's individuals "reject organizational mediation, seeking instead to have a direct impact upon matters that touch [their lives]. They "demand a high quality of direct participation and influence. They have the skills to lead, confer and discuss, and they are not content to be foot soldiers."

- They believe in leadership that is "bottom-up" rather than 'top-down,' preferring collective participation of average people to solve the problems.

The picture offered in these comments by Zuboff and Maxmin seems to describe the organization problems in our schools. Their remedy deserves consideration by school boards, administrators, teacher union leaders, and teacher leaders. They suggest that "old organizations have become sufficiently insulated and self-congratulatory to ignore the chasm that has formed between their practices, invented by mass society, and the new people it has spawned. . . . The new individuals are being blamed for the problems of the old organization when the facts suggest the opposite."[16]

In our discussion it takes the form of blaming veteran teachers for not accepting a buyout or for staying on "past their time" when the problems, such as budget cuts and staffing, are not of their making.

Yet, as Zuboff and Maxmin say, "Letting go of the past is painful. . . . People know how to operate in the system that already exists. They know how to compete and how to succeed in that system. Changing the deep structure of a system is threatening to everyone. There will be new winners and losers, new skills to learn, new ranking rules. These fears are compounded by the fact that many people have invested their entire careers in the old structures. . . . Change belittles their lifetime achievement. It diminishes all that they have sacrificed."[17]

Zuboff and Maxmin also say that another reason people avoid deep structure change "involves the relationships and commitments that people have developed both inside and outside the system. Individuals frequently find it difficult to change because they are afraid of disappointing the people closest to them, such as marital partners or professional colleagues. If a person has been valued by important others, he tends to fear the loss of that positive regard if he undergoes change and possibly develops new directions."[18]

In our discussion this can explain why some skilled veteran teachers, whose first choice is to remain in the classroom, may end up taking a buyout, because either their spouse or partner wants them to spend more time with the family or because they don't want to disappoint (and risk the wrath of) younger colleagues who need them to retire and create job openings for them.

Finally, Zuboff and Maxmin go to the heart of my argument that we need new leadership and mentoring career models and roles for veterans in which they serve as advocates, supporters, and colleagues. They suggest that what is needed now in our organizations are employee advocates "who possess the most extensive repertoire of tacit, as well as explicit, knowledge about the individuals [they support] . . . successful advocates [who] will have earned the trust of [these] individuals over time through the efficacy of their support. . . . Advocates gain power with the trust they hold but only to the extent that the individuals they support are themselves empowered by their efforts. If advocates leave, . . . they take these vital repositories of trust. This requires a new emphasis on the critical importance of retention and the search for new forms of remuneration."[19]

Skilled veteran teachers who are given the opportunity to serve as leaders, mentors, trainers, and supportive colleagues can fill the role of advocate that Zuboff and Maxmin describe. As Zuboff and Maxmin suggest, if the leadership in the schools promotes a plan to encourage these advocates to retire, they will lost these vital repositories of trust. What is needed is a new model that emphasizes the important of retention and remuneration, as in the case of Lori Gordon and Lauren Koster at PS 35, living examples of Zuboff and Maxmin's advocate model.

The focus of chapter 4 is to demonstrate why Zuboff and Maxmin's "advocate" role and Dychtwald's "mentoring, coaching, and training" roles are examples of the new "freedom to work" models that are emerging in our organizations. Many workers, including teachers, want to remain in the work-force past retirement age. Overall, they are highly skilled, healthy, energetic and not ready to leave a workplace they have helped build and sustain. They are forging a new workplace model, "freedom to work," that is replacing the outdated "freedom not to work" paradigm of the late twentieth century, a time when the goal of many workers was to retire to a life of leisure. As Zuboff and Maxmin say, people have new dreams now.

I have had firsthand experience with Zuboff and Maxmin's "advocate" role and Dychtwald's "mentoring, coaching, and training" role, as I describe in my book *An Administrator's Guide to Better Teacher Mentoring*. I was a professional with "new dreams" working in a large, overcrowded junior high school with many low-achieving students from poor neighborhoods. The principal, George Forbes, like so many principals in our large secondary schools, was often overwhelmed with student discipline problems, curriculum issues, and efforts to maintain a positive school climate that was always at risk of deteriorating. He literally had no time to mentor and support novice, mid-career, and veteran staff in need of improvement.

He needed an employee "advocate" who could earn the trust of the staff and empower them to change the deep culture of the school, by dreaming new dreams and demanding a high quality of direct participation and influence, to help them begin to believe that they, the teachers, had the resources and practical know-how to solve the problems in their school community.

Here is an excerpt from the book, describing how I became that advocate with my skills to lead, confer, and discuss. I was able to serve as a key player in the formation of a teacher training center with the goal of involving the entire staff in providing mentoring, coaching, training, and support for each other, using staff members as the primary source of intervention, not experts from outside.

Engaging teachers one by one on their own turf can play a major role in break-ing down resistance and opening up new, exciting doors for teacher renewal such as mentoring. I learned this lesson the hard way when I helped found and became director of the Bay Shore Public Schools-Stony Brook University Teacher Center in Bay Shore, New York. Here is my story and the personal anecdotes that were so important to me in my personal and professional life. It was an experience that inspired me to study and explore a variety of helping interventions for teachers, such as mentoring.

The evolvement of the center and my interest in teacher development, how the aging process affects veteran teachers, and how to overcome teachers' resis-tance to change began with my receiving my PhD from Syracuse University. I was excited about returning to the junior high school from which I was on leave for two years.

My dream was to start a unique teacher training center. I envisioned a center that would offer workshops during the school day that teachers, support staff and administrators could attend on their lunch breaks and during free periods. My vision was that the majority of workshops would be led by the school staff, with outside resources such as faculty at Stony Brook University also on board as workshop presenters.

Teachers who volunteered to lead workshops would be released from their teaching duties for the day. A grant from the university would enable the school to hire substitute teachers as replacements. The plan was for teachers to offer their workshops at each of the three faculty lunch periods and be available during the other periods for informal conversations with interested faculty.

My initial goal was to encourage teachers to decide on what workshops would help them to be more effective in the classroom. It was a homegrown effort specifically designed to meet the needs of teachers at the junior high, a reversal of the usual staff development offerings, which usually involved in-service workshops focused on meeting the goals and mission of the entire school district.

This was an exciting idea that was given full support by my principal, George Forbes. He understood that the project could have a major impact on improving the morale and effectiveness of teachers. Teaching at the junior high was not easy. The community had more than its share of low-income and at-risk kids. Forbes, a former counselor and school psychologist, knew the staff needed an infusion of new ideas and training and that the center might be the vehicle for change. He understood that he couldn't take on such a project himself.

Forbes told me, "I am so busy with everyday crises I have no time for staff development. I am hoping your experience at Syracuse can help us out in the area of teacher renewal. And I like the idea that you have cultivated a relationship with Stony Brook University. That relationship gives us some credibility with the district office, the school board and the teachers' union. Maybe we are in the beginning of offering courses here toward a master's degree and certification. Wouldn't that be great for our teachers? Save them from having to take courses at night at some faraway campus."

The forward in this book is dedicated to Forbes. He could see opportunity for change and knew to get out of the way. Forbes reduced the demands of my student assistance counseling job, allowing me a half day to help set up the center.

Leading a successful education reform effort, such as opening a teacher center or mentoring program, cannot be accomplished without having the time and support necessary to get the job done well. School administrators are so involved in a number of complex leadership issues that they simply don't have the time to lead and sell staff development programs.

Yes, they need to be involved on a number of levels, such as gaining funding, selling the program to district administration, developing support from key teacher and union leaders, and serving as a political cover for the program when it comes under attack. They know the political world they inhabit and understand how to leverage a good idea, but they don't have the time to put together all the nuts and bolts.

George Forbes understood his role and what he could and could not do and was so secure in himself that he was able to delegate his staff development role to me. Why did it seem a no-brainer to him? We had established a level of trust between us. He knew I was interested in developing the center, not in becoming the next principal or building a resume so I could move on and become a teacher center guru.

We were both committed to the job at hand—improving the professional lives of teachers, improving the school climate for students and parents, and affirming members of the support staff whose helping roles were often taken for granted. Secretaries, custodians, cafeteria and hall monitors, and teachers' aides are seldom given positive feedback for all the help they give to students.

George Forbes selflessly turned over part of his role to me and as my mentor freed me to do what I did best—listen, engage, involve, support and help others. Like me, Forbes enjoyed helping others to shine their light; he was a mentor in the truest sense of the word.

Many administrators care deeply for their teachers but are left with very little time to really supervise them, especially the veteran teachers. To commit to more intense supervision requires a major, often personal, commitment that most administrators can't sustain. There must be some element of identifying with a failing teacher that makes them put aside pressing issues and act to help a teacher failing and being left behind.

George Forbes understood that reality and acted unselfishly to utilize my experience and skills to help teachers. It's not easy for an administrator to have such an ego. It's a job in which one is usually on the defensive.

Giving up part of one's role and duties doesn't come easily. As a result, what we have in most schools is an organization that is not ready and set to respond to teachers heading toward the margins, whether they be veterans or novices.[20]

The three major sources of intervention—colleagues, guidance counselors or psychologists, and administrators—all have other roles. Colleagues are not trained to help; guidance counselors and psychologists have no defined role; administrators are too overwhelmed. In our current school organization, their roles have been reduced to those of observers. They are not responsible for the problem or to be blamed for it.

What is clear is the urgent need to develop new mechanisms in the school organization—such as mentoring—that can provide the kind of support highly functioning teachers need to continue on a successful path. There is no mystery here in terms of what is needed. Many of our schools are stuck in a no-win situation, always playing a game of catch-up when it comes to giving novice and veteran teachers what they need to be more effective. Let us not be fooled by the illusion that this is an easy path. But it is a path of necessity.

In smaller, leaner, less crowded schools such as PS 35, the boss, the principal, such as Graciela Navarro, whom I describe in chapter 5, can take on an advocate role, mentoring, coaching, and training role. Google is pioneering such a model. *New York Times* writer Adam Brant reports that "in early 2009, statisticians at Google embarked on a plan code-named Project Oxygen. The mission was to devise something far more important to the future of Google, Inc. than its next search algorithm or app. They wanted to build better bosses."[21]

Bryant reports that "Project Oxygen started with some basic assumptions. People typically leave a company for one of three reasons or a combination of them. The first is that they don't feel connected to the mission of the company or sense that their work matters. The second is that they don't really like or respect their co-workers. The third is that they have a terrible boss—and this was the biggest variable." Google performance reviews are done quarterly.

Project Oxygen teams also found "managers had a much greater impact on employees' performance and how they felt about their job than any other factor." Laszlo Bock, Google's vice president for people operations said, "Our best managers have teams that perform better, are retained better, are happier, do everything better. So the biggest controllable factor that we could see was the quality of the manager and how they sort of made things happen. The question we then asked was, 'What if every manager was that good?' And then you start saying, 'Well, what makes them that good? And how do you do it?'"

In gathering data the "people analytics" teams analyzed performance reviews, feedback surveys and nominations for top manager awards. The teams produced what might be called the "eight habits of highly effective Google managers." The team findings suggest that for much of its history, particularly in the early years, Google has taken a pretty simple approach to management. Leave it alone. "Let the engineers do their stuff. If they become stuck, they'll ask their bosses, whose deep technical expertise propelled them into management in the first place."

However, the "people analytic" teams found that technical expertise ranked last among Google's big eight. "What employees valued most were even-keeled bosses who made time for one-on-one meetings, who helped people puzzle through problems by asking questions, not dictating answers, and who took an interest in employees' lives and careers."

Here is Bryant's edited list of the eight group behaviors, in order of importance:

1. Be a good coach.
2. Empower your teams and don't micromanage.
3. Express interest in team members' success and personal well-being.

4. Don't be a sissy; be productive and results oriented.
5. Be a good communicator and listen to your team.
6. Help your employees with career development.
7. Have a clear vision and strategy for the team.
8. Have key technical skills so you can advise the team.

Bryant reports that "Mr. Brock says he is particularly struck by the simplicity of the rules and the fact that applying them doesn't require a personality transplant as a manger. . . . 'You don't actually need to change who the person is. What it means is that is I'm a manager and I want to get better and I want more out of my people and I want to be happier, two of the most important things I can do are just to make sure I have some time for them and to be consistent. And that's more important than doing the rest of the stuff.'"[22]

Zuboff and Maxmin might categorize the findings of Project Oxygen as an example of looking elsewhere, over there in the darkness, rather than under the light of the lamp post, finding that employees, not the model expert boss, have the resources and practical know-how to solve many problems. They do this best when they are given a boss, or principal, who will listen to them, get to know them on a personal as well as professional basis, take an interest in their career development and reward their successes.

Occasionally a wholesale transformation in a system's deep structure is needed. I believe the current budget battles in our schools are providing such a change in the deep structures of our school organizations.

As I will describe in chapters 4, 5, and 6, the change is on. Our challenge, as Maynard Keyes suggests, is to "escape from the habitual modes of thought and expression. The difficulty lies not in the new ideas but in escaping the old ones."

NOTES

1. Marc Freedman, *Encore: Finding Work That Matters in the Second Half of Life* (New York, NY: Perseus Books, 2008), 80.
2. Bob Silverblatt, "Tracking the Recession: Buyouts Lure 9,000 Workers into Retirement," *Stateline.org*, August 18, 2009, http://stateline.org/live/details/story?contenId=418011 (accessed October 15, 2010).
3. Joe Light, "When the New Temp Happens to Be the Boss," *Wall Street Journal*, February 28, 2011, http://online.wsj.com/article/SB1000142405274870469290457616 64432492145652.html
4. Light, "When the New Temp."
5. Mark Miller, "Laid-Off Older Workers Face Multiple Obstacles," *Newsday*, March 5, 2011, B7.

6. Sloan Center on Aging and Work, "Older Adults Struggle in Job Search," *Sloan Center News*, November 16, 2010, http://www.bc.edu/research/agingandwork/archive_news/2010/2010-11-16.htm (accessed January 21, 2011).

7. William L. Fibkins, "Why Am I Looking for Work When I Don't Have To?" in The Dark and Sometimes Humorous Side of Retirement and Aging (unpublished manuscript, 2009).

8. Miller, "Laid-Off Older Workers."

9. Ken Dychtwald, Tamara J. Erickson, and Robert Morison, *Workforce Crisis: How to Beat the Coming Shortage of Skills and Talents* (Boston, MA: Harvard Business School Press, 2006), 45.

10. Dychtwald et al., *Workforce Crisis*, 35–36.

11. Dychtwald et al., *Workforce Crisis*, 14.

12. Dychtwald et al., *Workforce Crisis*, 25–26, 38–39, 40–42.

13. Dychtwald et al., *Workforce Crisis*, 45

14. Shoshona Zuboff and James Maxmin, *The Support Economy: Why Corporations are Failing Individuals and the Next Episode of Capitalism* (New York, NY: Penguin Putnam, Inc., 2002), 18.

15. Zuboff and Maxmin, *The Support Economy*, 19, 21, 23, 25, 108, 109

16. Zuboff and Maxmin, *The Support Economy*, 116, 117.

17. Zuboff and Maxmin, *The Support Economy*, 283

18. Zuboff and Maxmin, *The Support Economy*, 284

19. Zuboff and Maxmin, *The Support Economy*, 368

20. William F. Fibkins, *An Administrator's Guide to Better Teacher Mentoring*, 2nd ed. (Lanham, MD: Rowman & Littlefield Education, 2011), 180, 181, 186.

21. Adam Bryant, "The Quest to Build a Better Boss," *New York Times*, March 13, 2011.

22. Bryant, "The Quest to Build a Better Boss."

Chapter 4

Older Workers Are Needed in the Workforce

Public Policy and Private Practice Encourages Them to Retire

Marc Freedman, CEO of Civic Ventures, a think tank on boomers' work and social purpose, suggests that in 1950 half of the men over sixty-five remained in the workforce. By 2000 the number was less than 18 percent. At the same time, older adults emerged as the biggest consumers of leisure-time activities in America. Soon the goal of retirement was replaced by a new dream—early retirement.

A half century later America finds itself in the midst of a demographic revolution, propelled by the aging of 78 million baby boomers. By 2030 these individuals will make up between 20 and 25 percent of the overall population. This gift of longevity is behind the shift in the way people think about retirement. In 1900 the average American lived to the age of forty-seven. Today that number is seventy-seven and rising. That's long enough for retirees to get bored. How much golf can you play?

As a result, now people think of retirement as a final stage of life. While much about this evolution of goals and purpose in this period of life remains unclear, a central defining feature is emerging. It is work. The vast majority of boomers plan to continue working full-time, part-time, paid or unpaid in their so-called retirement years. According to a recent study by AARP, nearly 80 percent of boomers are planning to continue in paid labor during their sixties and seventies.

The new generation of aging boomers seems poised to swap that old dream of freedom from work for a new one built around the freedom to work—in new ways, on new terms, to new ends.

Freedman also suggests that inklings of such a vision are already appearing. For example, a recent ad campaign from Home Depot and AARP announces a new partnership to recruit older workers. The campaign beckons them to trade retirement for a new vision of what work can be. The slogan? "Passion Never Retires."

This trend is welcome news. We now know that work is good for aging individuals themselves, for their health as well as their wallets. At the same time, the nation faces the prospect of a labor shortage in many areas over the coming decade. Now that millions of baby boomers are turning sixty, we need to create an aging America that swaps the old leisure ideal for one that balances the joys and responsibilities of engagement across the lifespan. That could produce a society that works better for all generations.[1]

A 2010 Gallup poll reveals that America's projected retirement age has gradually increased over the past fifteen years with more than one-third of non-retirees today saying they will retire after age sixty-five as compared with 12 percent in 1995. Gallup first asked non-retired Americans, "At what age do you expect to retire?" in 1995 and has asked that question every year since 2002.

There has been a clear shift in retirement intentions over this period. Now, sixteen years later, Americans' retirement intentions are more dispersed. Thirty-four percent say they will retire after age sixty-five, while the percentage saying they will retire before that age has shrunk to 29 percent and 27 percent say they will retire at sixty-five.

This poll suggests that many societal and economic forces may be causing this shift in retirement projections. The baby boomer generation is now approaching the traditional retirement age. The expectations this large demographic group about the nature and rewards of work differ from the expectations of those who came before. Additionally, the workforce has faced a major recession in the past few years, perhaps increasing the perceived value of a job, given decreasing expectations of money being available in retirement accounts.

The Gallup poll analysis of this data indicates it could be good news for the American economy if workers do follow through on their intentions as measured in Gallup surveys and continue to postpone retirement. Some economists have projected a need for additional labor to keep the economy going in years ahead and older workers could help fill that need. Also, the longer Americans work, the more they contribute and the less they drain from the Social Security and Medicare systems, good for the federal deficit situation. The impact of working beyond traditional retirement age on individual well-being is less clear. Some could argue that working helps older Americans stay active, mentally engaged and fulfilled.[2]

Marc Miller argues that the topic of aging in America often prompts discussion and worry about how we'll manage our graying country. Miller points out that author Ted Fishman puts those questions into a broader context in his new book, *Shock of Gray*. He reviewed Fishman's findings and shared his review in an article, "Our Graying Will Reshape Our World."

According to Miller, Fishman suggests it will be more common for people in their late sixties and seventies to work. It will also be common for older workers to have living parents to tend to. The workforce over fifty will grow to three times its current size, but the number of younger workers will stay nearly constant. Virtually all the expansion in the United States workforce will be in the upper age range.

Fishman says that currently the standard retirement ages in every developed country—when workers can start to get social security—are higher than the ages at which people actually leave their primary jobs. People are encouraged to leave. They are bought out, made redundant, or left in the cold when their jobs leave.

For American workers at mid-career, they must try to ensure that their labor isn't devalued. They need to make sure they have a good inventory of skills and a strong social network before they find themselves in an employment crisis. Fishman argues that the best way to avoid that crisis is to focus on developing differential skills. He says we have a large group of workers who haven't kept their skills current.[3]

Fishman's assessment helps crystallize the argument for retaining our highly skilled veteran teachers. Many veteran teachers have made a great effort to improve their skills at each stage of their career and not let their labor be devalued. They have embodied a good inventory of skills into their daily work and kept their skills current. It makes no sense to subject them to a management policy in which they are encouraged to leave their jobs by being bought out, left in the cold, or isolated because they are deemed redundant.

That is the path poorly skilled and incompetent teachers have carved out for themselves over the life of their careers. They let their labor be devalued because of their lack of commitment to developing the necessary new skills needed to be good teachers. Their path has been one of counting the days to retirement while not appearing so incompetent as to risk being fired. But they are redundant to any healthy organization and an early buyout is the right choice for them as they close in on retirement, a buyout that will make way for a cadre of new teachers.

Education leaders need to be careful, as the wise saying goes, not to throw out the baby with the bath water. They cannot afford to adopt a one-size-fits-all attitude when it comes to crunch time.

In terms of the impact of working beyond retirement age on keeping workers mentally engaged, Gina Kolata reports that taking early retirement may retire memory. Two economists, Robert Willis, a professor of economics at the University of Michigan, and Susann Rohwedder, associate director of

Rand Center for the Study of Aging, suggest in their paper "Mental Retirement" that the earlier people retire, the more quickly their memories decline. The implication, the economists and others say, is that there really seems to be something to the "use it or lose it" notion. If people want to preserve their memories and reasoning abilities, they may have to keep active.

Willis and Rohwedder's research also indicates that there is evidence that social skills and personality skills—getting up in the morning, dealing with people, knowing the value of being prompt and trustworthy—are also important. They go hand in hand with the work environment.

Willis and Rohwedder's research also adds some support for the argument in this book for successful veteran teachers being given the option of remaining in the workforce. They found a straight-line relationship between the percentage of people in a country who are working at age sixty to sixty-four and their performance on memory tests. The longer people in a country keep working, the better, as a group, they do on tests when they are in their early sixties.

In contrast, they found that countries with earlier retirement ages often have incentives such as the early buyouts that encourage people to leave work at a younger age. Willis and Rohwedder's research involved data from the United States, England, and eleven other European countries.[4]

Working longer appears to have some positive effect on people if they want to preserve their memories and reasoning abilities. The earlier people retire, the more quickly their memories decline.

The Texas Office of Aging Policy and Information report "Aging Matters" says that as the baby boomer population approaches retirement age, there is a need to more closely evaluate the impact of demographics on the Texas workforce. The Texas Department of Aging Vision Statement on an Aging Texas indicates that older people should have the opportunity to secure employment and education. While some Texans will retire, others will choose to continue working and pursue new careers. Many middle- and low-income older adults will have to work out of financial necessity.

The U.S. Department of Labor projects continued labor force growth. The percentage of workers aged forty-five and older will increase from 33 percent of the labor force in 1998 to 40 percent in 2008, adding nearly 1.7 million workers to this age group. Over the same period, those aged twenty-five to forty-four will decline as a percentage of the labor force, from 51 percent to 44 percent, resulting in three million fewer workers in this bracket. The aging of the population will substantially affect certain occupations and industries. Labor force needs may go unmet unless older workers are retained.

In terms of our discussion of the need to retain highly skilled veteran teachers, the report says that one of the industries most affected will be educational services. Employees in the educational services tend to retire earlier because they have benefit plans that provide the maximum economic benefit for those who retire at the earliest possible age of eligibility.

According to the Department of Labor, elementary and secondary teachers, along with educational administrators, are among the top ten occupations with the greatest replacement needs due to persons over the age of forty-five leaving the occupation from 1998 to 2008.

Also key to our discussion, the report suggests that older adults can help offset the projected decline in labor force growth, but public policies and private practices often overlook their potential contributions and encourage them to retire prematurely. Many people leave the workforce long before their health makes it necessary. The report concludes by echoing a major theme of this book: "There are many private and public incentives to retire early and a lack of policies to encourage older workers to keep working."[5]

In an interview with *New York Times* reporter Marci Alboher, Marc Freedman, CEO of Encore and Civic Ventures, spoke to the issue of why employers aren't helping to retain older workers. He said, "Employers need to recognize, particularly those facing talent shortages, that there is more than one place to look when filling these gaps. While many young people have an enormous amount to offer, there is another vast and growing pool of talent and commitment, older workers. Employers need to correct some misconceptions. They often assume people in their fifties and sixties have one foot out the door. But an accumulation of evidence supports the fact that turnover is less with this population than with young people. So it's worth investing in these individuals."[6]

The need to reinvent retirement is the theme of a special report by Richard Adler, vice president for research and development for Civic Ventures. Adler says, "Among the examples cited in the article of the consequences of losing these unique resources, when the Russians approached International Harvester to build a factory, there was no one left who knew how it was done."[7]

However, some change is on the horizon. Adler says that some employers have begun to recognize the need to encourage older workers to keep working. As an example, Volkswagen has abandoned its previous policies that encouraged early retirement and now believes that its older workers are indispensable to keeping the company competitive and profitable.

In his book *Fifty Plus: Give Meaning and Purpose to the Best Time of Your Life*, Bill Novelli, CEO of AARP, adds to the notion of reinventing retirement for older workers. He says,

For the first time in history, long life isn't a rarity. Two-thirds of the people who ever reached the age of 65 are alive today. What's more, 65 isn't even old anymore; most of us can count on another eighteen years or so after that, and more than half of us will live past 90. The fastest growing segment of the population is those 85 and older. . . . We have a growing older population that by and large is vital and active and possesses great intellectual wealth. But we have not structured a social model to optimize their continued involvement. . . . Many, in fact, fear this future.[8]

Novelli goes on to say,

Retirement is being reinvented right before our eyes. As more people live longer and healthier lives, they are searching for ways to continue contributing to society while finding personal fulfillment in their own lives. . . . Regardless of their activities, they don't see live after 50 as a time to shift into neutral. . . . [However] "retirement planning has not kept up with the startling increase in longevity or the expectations of an active lifestyle. Making it easier for older people to find and hold onto jobs is one solution to the problem. Many people want or need to work into their so-called retirement years. . . . In 2012 the "baby bust" generation that follows the boomers will, in all probability, be unable to fill all the available jobs. Some enlightened companies, aware of the looming shortfall and eager to retain the skills and experience of their most mature workers, are encouraging the 50+ generation to stay on the job. But others are still pushing the notion of early retirement or simply saying good-bye to older workers. This myopia is bad for all those who want to continue working, contributing and earning the money they need to live comfortably in the next stage of their lives, and it's detrimental to the . . . country as a whole. Fortunately, change is afoot as self-interested employers increasingly understand the folly of denying themselves the value that older workers add to the workplace. "Aging in place" is the dream of most people—and enabling older people to remain in their communities as they age can benefit the community as well. The wit and wisdom that comes with a lifetime of experiences enriches life for everyone.[9]

Novelli reminds us that "staying on the job doesn't have to mean toiling away forty or more hours a week. While many . . . intend to do just that, others are reducing the number of hours or days on the job or accepting a cut in pay for a new job with fewer responsibilities." "Phased retirement," where employees gradually lessen their employment as they approach retirement is becoming a favored option. Workers who take this route, are more likely to view their jobs favorably and may remain in the workforce longer.[10]

The importance of rethinking how to reinvent retirement by suggesting different work models for older workers becomes a critical factor when, as Novelli suggests, "the largest part of the U.S. workforce is made up of knowledge workers, and more than 4 million members of that workforce are between the ages of 65 and 74. By 2031 49.9 million workers will be at or past the traditional retirement age of 65. Looking at the aging workforce from a different vantage point, by 2020, 20 percent of America's workers will pass 55 and over the following seven years the 55-to-64-year-old segment will expand by 55 percent."[11]

This is important because the United States is facing a shortage of younger employees, due to the lower birthrate that followed the baby boom.

Baby boomers who want or need to work past the retirement age should be allowed to fill the gap.

Many people want to keep full-time jobs well into their seventies, a right guaranteed to most of us by the longstanding laws against age discrimination. Novelli suggests that eventually "a majority of boomers will be working in their later years—and the nation's employers, many of which traditionally looked for ways to show older workers the door, will accelerate the change in policies and practices aimed at retaining and recruiting mature workers."[12]

Employing skilled mature workers appears to be a winning strategy for employers. For example, Novelli shared an analysis of data from an AARP survey of what employers thought of employees over the age of fifty. The results indicate that employers see people over fifty as: "Being committed to doing quality work; getting along well with others; having solid performance records; possessing basic skills in reading, writing, and math; being dependable in a crisis; and exhibiting loyalty and dedication to the company."

And Novelli quotes Alicia Munnell, director of the Center for Retirement Research at Boston College: "Increased employment of older workers seems like a natural solution. Employers will have to change their hiring and retention policies if they want to attract these highly productive older individuals."[13]

As I suggest, there is little talk of new roles and incentives or tailoring assignments to give veteran teachers a reason to stay in their schools. They can serve not only as leaders and a stabilizing force, but also as a source of experience, knowledge and information in the school community. They can be sharing their knowledge as experts in the field, helping to provide novice teachers with the skills they need to survive instead of failing and then getting fired or quitting.

The effort to retain novice teachers grows more problematic each day, not only because we are not utilizing skilled veteran teachers to mentor and guide them but because the pool of younger teachers is shrinking year by year. It is approaching a national emergency as the school workforce is being drained of both younger and older workers. As Novelli suggests, despite the looming labor shortage, not every sector and every company is seeking older workers. Right now the public schools unfortunately fit that description.

Zuboff and Maxmin remind us that "typically people in organizations do not see what's coming. Events are not read as indications people should change what they are doing or how they are thinking. On the contrary, challenging events are often regarded as a signal that people should do the same thing they already know how to do, even more assiduously than before."[14]

This observation translates to the public schools continuing to support the shortsighted process of *out with the old, in with the new* to balance the budget However, crunch time is coming soon. There is a shortage of younger workers, including teachers. At the same time, many younger teachers are quitting. Principals, particularly in our large secondary schools, are overwhelmed and have little time to mentor and support younger teachers. Skilled veteran teachers are the logical, only, choice to intervene and help save and nurture the careers of younger teachers. But they are being bought out.

The staffing system in our public schools is deteriorating rapidly. But, as Zuboff and Maxmin suggest, school district leaders are looking where the light happens to be shining, not in the darkness, not seeing that the answer to the survival of novice teachers and the school district is right in front of their eyes—retaining veteran teachers to intervene. A staffing emergency looms but things haven't gotten bad enough to call for the lifeboats. Not just yet. School districts keep bailing water, but they are running out of bailers. The old-timers and younger crew members have left the ship, replaced by new hires with no experience.

In their book *Working Longer: New Strategies for Managing, Training and Retaining Older Workers*, Rothwell, Sterns, Spokus, and Reaser raise the issue of the perils that companies face when their workforce is largely composed of young, inexperienced workers and absent the knowledge of older workers. They cite the example of NASA in the 1960s putting a man on the moon. and how today it no longer knows how to get there. That's because the engineers who designed the space program were sold on an early retirement to cut costs.

The public schools are not alone in failing to promote new strategies to retain mature workers. Rothwell et al. cite a survey conducted by the Society for Human Resource Management (SHRM) that found these statistics:

- 59 percent of companies do not recruit older workers
- 65 percent of companies have no retention practices
- 71 percent of companies have no specific provisions for benefits for older workers[15]

Part of the problem in retaining mature workers lies with the way workers themselves view their careers. This holds true especially for teachers. The culture in which teachers work and their own sense of a *career* usually involves retiring in their fifties. Early retirement simply speeds up that process. It's the way things are done, a process drilled into their brains and souls from day one. In my observations as a teacher reformer, I found that in faculty room conversations the topic of retirement ranks much higher than how to continue to grow one's career, even for younger and mid-career teachers.

Given this culture, it's difficult for teachers to even consider a different career path or new roles that involve staying on board as leaders, mentor, coaches, or trainers. "Get out as soon as you can" seems to be the light guiding the daily lives of most teachers. This is the career path teachers know. Of course, this should not come as a surprise. Other career models for them to emulate simply do not exist in most school communities. There are no role models as exemplified by leader/mentors such as Lori Gordon and Lauren Koster at New York City PS 35, whom I describe in chapter 5, and my own experience at Bay Shore Junior High, which I identified in earlier chapters.

Currently the school organizations anoint only a few select educators as dispensers of knowledge—the principal, assistant principal, and department chairs in secondary schools. In many schools' organizational charts there is no staffing line, position, and clear-cut role for great teachers. There are many highly skilled teachers like Koster and Gordon who embody vast knowledge and experience, but they are sitting on the sidelines or with one foot out the door, never realizing how talented they really are.

The only visible career model teachers know and understand is that of older teachers retiring when they reach a certain age. It's the way teachers in general manage their careers. Self-management of one's career, in which the individual teacher, not the group, decides what he or she needs to grow and whether to stay or retire, barely exists in our school culture. In my research I have found that the group culture is winning out in deciding these issues for teachers. Also, as Zuboff and Maxmin point out, individuals frequently find it hard to change because they are afraid of disappointing the people closest to them.

Even if we create new roles such as teacher leaders and mentors in our school organizations, it's going to take courageous work and risk-taking teachers such as Gordon and Koster to leave their peer group and assume leadership roles, no longer being comfortable, protected members of a group. They must be willing to opt for change and risk new directions that require a high level of individuality and self-direction. These new leaders will need benefits and remuneration to reward their efforts to bring about and model organizational transformation and change.

Rothwell et al. suggest that older workers of the future may be more valued for being more adaptable and knowledgeable. A "new careerism has led to employees being more critical in self-analysis, more assertive in seeking feedback, and more likely to refuse transfer and promotions that subvert career goals as they envision them."[16] I would add that they will be more likely to refuse being bought out when their career goals involve staying on as leaders, mentors, coaches, and trainers.

Gordon F. Shea and Adolf Hassen, in their book *The Older Worker Advantage*, add to our discussion about the need to retain older workers, suggesting that "we are increasingly dependent on older workers to produce for, and help manage, our society. Above all we need a more balanced look at our workforce if we are to gain maximum advantage from each or our age segments in the decades ahead."[17] In terms of the school environment, that means we are going to need the skills and input of all our teachers— novice, mid-career, and veteran.

As Shea and Hassen suggest, workers of different ages contribute different skills. Accordingly, schools need to change their ways of doing business and encourage older teachers who need or want to remain employed. By giving them early retirement, we are wasting their knowledge and abilities as mentors.

Changing and remedying the past and present practices of management toward older workers will not be easy. As we see in the culture of our public schools, older workers are often targeted as obsolete, a late career label that paints all veteran teachers with one negative brush, subtly blaming them for hanging on to their jobs too long while their skills rapidly diminish. This charge ignores the reality that there are many highly skilled veterans who are great teachers. I have observed many of these teachers firsthand. I have also observed some veteran teachers who are on the road to obsolescence, and in the school culture, they are the ones who attract much of the negative attention given to older teachers. The news about problems caused by a minority of teachers always wins out over the news about the successes of great teachers. Check your newspaper.

There is a stereotype in the school culture that older teachers are all alike; this defies observation, logic, and common sense. The stereotyping of older workers tends to treat them with a package approach when it comes to work issues. It's a one-size-fits-all approach that allows for no individual differentiation for older teachers in terms of skills and knowledge acquired, leadership roles, success rate, performance, attendance, self-directed learning, and so forth.

As a result, when older teachers begin to head toward the margins of school life, their problems tend to grow worse because they receive little or no support to change. It's often a sink-or-swim, you're-on-your-own culture in the public schools, particularly at the secondary level. There is no early warning, flashing red light in the current package approach, no individual differentiation for teachers, for good or bad. It's a band of brothers all marching to the same tune, until one falls. Falling teachers get the help they need only by falling, so no one in the school community can miss or avoid their plight. Often it comes too late.

The package approach dims the cries for help of falling teachers and also the motivation and readiness on the part of school community members to come to their aid. Principals are too busy. Some colleagues say their job is to teach, not to help. That's the job of the administration. Other colleagues, who may want to help, feel they lack the skills to intervene. For many failing teachers, young, mid-career, and older, there is no lifeline of mentoring as provided by PS 35's Lori Gordon and Lauren Koster. There is a world with two different cultures, one for students and one for teachers. One culture prides itself on individual differences, interventions, and support for students. For teachers it's a one-size-fits-all culture that says "keep marching, don't fall." Teachers in this culture don't have problems, don't fail. Only students do that.

It then comes as no surprise that the promise that mentoring offers comes too late. This was the case with Harry Walker, whom I describe in *An Administrator's Guide to Better Teacher Mentoring*. As Harry grew older he crossed the boundary from being a successful teacher and coach to being a teacher whose classes were undisciplined and out of control, whose behaviors frightened some peers and angered others, who felt he was giving the staff a bad name. While some staff voiced sympathy for Harry, most of the faculty wanted him out.

Harry's exit could provide relief of a different kind as well. There were looming budget cuts in the school district, which meant that some novice teachers could lose their jobs. An early buyout for Harry could create new job opportunities for the at-risk teachers.[18]

Shea and Hassen put the blame for worker obsolescence on management. They say "personal obsolescence often reflects inadequacies in the work environment that contribute to the insufficient use or misuse of human talent. . . . When older employees see no chance for advancement or challenge, they may respond by putting in just enough effort to keep their jobs. There is little evidence that older workers are not interested in advancement or in a particular challenge, but they may withdraw from active involvement, become dispirited and lose energy if they believe their aspirations are being smothered."[19]

Whether or not failed aspirations were the cause of Harry Walker's descent, it is a state of mind that can and does affect veteran teachers who reach a place in their careers that offers no risks, no new challenges, no opportunities to create new dreams or no new career roles that might enable them to share their knowledge and skills as mentoring colleagues. The only way to move is to get out, by retiring, taking a buyout or, as in Harry's case, by acting out and performing so poorly that the school district is forced to pull the plug on his career.

That is the career model teachers see for themselves in the public schools, a model that Shea and Hassen say leads to older professionals not investing time in learning new skills because there is no reason to expect they will be able to use them. Who can blame them? As in all relations, personal and professional, things can only get worse if there is little support and guidance to change things for the better.

Problems can also arise when the principal becomes overwhelmed and consequently burned out, tired, and unmotivated to make any special effort to help employees succeed. This situation can arise, as in the case of Lori Gordon and Lauren Koster at PS 35 (as I will describe in chapter 5, a living example of Zuboff and Maxmin's advocate model), despite the fact that many older, experienced employees are available to share the load. The common belief of supervisors that they should do everything themselves wears them out and defeats them.

As I cited earlier in this chapter, my experience has shown me that inviting highly experienced older employees to help share the load may have few takers if the culture of the workplace is not changed. Mentors Lori Gordon and Lauren Koster are the exception, willing to take on a new role with all the risks involved. In today's school culture many highly skilled veteran teachers back off from new opportunities and are fearful of the possible charge by colleagues that they are getting "too big for their britches." They are viewed by their colleagues as stepping up and out of their teaching role by taking on a new career as a mentor or, as one teacher told me, "doing the job the principal should be doing."

The school culture makes the path for skilled veteran teachers taking on new roles even more complicated by fostering the assumption that these teachers cannot contribute anymore, that the future belongs to the young. But Sara Rix, in her book *Older Workers*, says that "those who argue in favor of divesting their workforce of older employees may overlook the cost of recruiting and retraining new workers. These costs may be minimal if unskilled workers are needed and available, but they can be substantial when highly experienced workers are necessary. . . . It may even be necessary to recruit several new workers to replace one retiring employee."[20]

As I say in chapters 5 and 6, we need to change the school culture so that we open up new doors and roles that can encourage the use of the skills and talents of the entire faculty—novice, mid-career, and veteran teachers—not leaving the problem solving to a small cadre of administrators, counselors, and department chairs.

Maybe then the Harry Walkers of the teaching world could be helped to change before it becomes too late. Maybe the one-size-fits-all package approach can finally be exposed as a major reason for limiting the individual differences, talents, and skills of teachers from every segment of the school staff. Intergenerational cooperation is in great demand as the young need the wisdom and experience of the elders and the elders need the energy, spirit, and risk-taking of the young.

Highly skilled veteran teachers are now going to have to rethink their career options and consider how to change the prevalent low-risk model of staying in one classroom your entire career and risk taking their place in new roles that offer greater leadership and responsibility. They must let their stars shine and their voice of knowledge, experience, and skills be heard. Wisdom is a much in-demand skill in our schools.

In sports lingo it's being the player who wants the ball to shoot when the basketball game is on the line or the baseball player who wants the bat in his hand when his team needs a big hit. What is needed is the player, the teacher, who is willing and able to take risks, not fear failure, and not hide in the crowd when individual action is needed, to be seen and known as someone who can deliver what is needed or at least make the best effort.

We need experienced, knowledgeable, highly skilled, committed, risk-taking and caring teachers from every segment of the school community if we are to help students improve their performance and learn to become caring, responsible, and contributing members of our society. We cannot accomplish this goal without our veteran teachers. We can't fight this war with a quarter of our army being furloughed or being forced to abandon the fight, seeking shelter far away from the battle that needs to be won.

As chapter 5 suggests, creating such a career path, in which veteran teachers can easily choose the freedom-to-work model and abandon the early retirement model will not be easy. But there are hopeful signs, lessons, and models emerging that we can follow.

Talia Milgrom-Elcott, a program officer in Urban Education for the Carnegie Corporation, says the National Bureau of Economics Research substantiated a school-level approach that suggests that in addition to talents, beliefs and the determination they bring to the job, teachers' success also depends on their individual experience in the system. "The more effective a teacher's colleagues, they more effective he or she is, and such spillovers tend to benefit less-experienced teachers the most."[21]

NOTES

1. Marc Freedman, "The Selling of Retirement, and How We Bought It," *Washington Post*, February 6, 2005, B01.

2. Frank Newport, "Americans' Projected Retirement Age Continues to Creep Up," April 26, 2010, http://www.gallup.com/poll/127514/Americans-Projected-Retirement-Age-Continues-Creep-Up.aspx (accessed October 26, 2010).

3. Mark Miller, "Our Graying Will Reshape the World," *Newsday*, February 19, 2011, B7.
4. Gina Kolata, "Taking Early Retirement May Retire Memory, Too," *New York Times*, October 12, 2010, D1.6.
5. Texas Office of Aging Policy and Information, *Workforce and Older Texans*, OAPI Policy Paper (Austin, TX: Texas Office of Aging Policy and Information, 2002), 1–3.
6. Marci Alboher, "Discovering Second Acts in Sustained Working Lives," *New York Times*, February 11, 2008, accessed October 16, 2010, http://www.nytimes .com/2008/02/11/jobs/1shift.html?ref=teach_for_America&pagewant
7. Richard Adler, "Special Report: Reinventing Retirement," *Civic Ventures*, December 2004, accessed October 18, 2010, http://www.civicventures.org/publications/articles/reinventing_retirement.cfm.
8. Bill Novelli, *Fifty Plus: Give Meaning and Purpose to the Best Time of Your Life* (New York, NY: St. Martin's Press, 2008), 11.
9. Novelli, *Fifty Plus*, 16–17.
10. Novelli, *Fifty Plus*, 88.
11. Novelli, *Fifty Plus*, 99
12. Novelli, *Fifty Plus*, 100
13. Novelli, *Fifty Plus*, 108.
14. Shoshona Zuboff and James Maxmin, *The Support Economy: Why Corporations are Failing Individuals and the Next Episode of Capitalism* (New York, NY: Penguin Putnam, Inc., 2002), 116
15. William J. Rothwell, Harvey Sterns, Diane Spokus, and Joel Reaser, *Working Longer: New Strategies for Managing, Training and Retaining Older Employees* (New York, NY: American Management Association, 2008) 9, 10.
16. Rothwell et al., *Working Longer*.
17. Gordon F. Shea and Adolf Hassen, *The Older Worker Advantage: Making the Most of Our Aging Workforce* (Westport, CT: Praeger Publishers, 2006), 11.
18. William L. Fibkins, *An Administrator's Guide to Better Teacher Mentoring* (Lanham, MD: Rowman & Littlefield Education, 2011) 188, 189.
19. Shea and Hassen, *The Older Worker Advantage*, 123.
20. Sara E. Rix, *Older Workers: Choice and Challenge* (Santa Barbara, CA: ABC-CLIO, Inc., 1990), 69.
21. Talia Milgrom-Elcott, *The Elusive Talent Strategy: An Excellent Teacher for Every Student in Every School*, A Carnegie Challenge Paper (New York, NY: The Carnegie Corporation of New York, 2011), 4.

Chapter 5

Resistance to Veteran Teachers Choosing the Freedom-to-Work Paradigm

Mikki Cichocki is a board member of the California Teachers' Association (CTA) and an educator in the Youth Services Program in the San Bernardino City Unified School District, an educator and teacher union representative who knows firsthand about teacher retirement incentives. She paints the current three-for-one epidemic in the stark, dark colors surrounding the retirement process of veteran teachers as they battle the onslaught of out-with-the-old, in-with-the-new thinking.

Cichocki reports that in her 2010 State of the State address, Michigan Governor Jennifer Granholm proposed retirement incentives for 39,000 eligible Michigan teachers and school personnel. She suggested that when "old teachers" retired, younger teachers could take their places. Unemployment rates would improve and college graduates would have an incentive to remain in the state. Retirees would have their pensions raised slightly, but those who refused the package would be penalized. Meanwhile President Obama is proposing fifty billion dollars for education focusing on teacher accountability: merit pay for teachers who raise test scores.

Ms. Cichocki is rightfully baffled by the goals of the Michigan plan in light of Mr. Obama's goals. Michigan wants its experienced teachers, many only in the early fifties, to get out of the way, thus newer teachers will not have the benefit of being mentored by the most experienced. To me it sounds like teacher accountability without being trained in how to be accountable.

Ms. Cichocki offers the wise analysis that demanding that teachers retire is a poor solution to the economic debacle. Out-with-the-old, in-with-the-new is not appropriate when it comes to educating kids. "Unfortunately," says Ms. Cichocki, "many believe in the stereotype that teachers morph over time into 'lounge lizards.' . . . Granted, bad teachers exist. But every profession has

57

its loafers. But by its very nature education demands that teachers keep up-to-date with current trends and strategies. . . . Suggesting that they no longer have something to contribute because they've accumulated thirty years of experience reeks of ageism."[1]

The slogan out-with-the-old, in-with-the-new captures the current battles going on in our schools. But who are the "new" teachers who want to land a job? The cohort of new would-be teachers is a mixed group. Cohort one consists of recent graduates of traditional teacher education programs. Cohort two are from nontraditional teacher education programs. For example, Teach for America, Troops-To-Teachers, made up of retired military personnel; IBM Transition to Teaching; Chicago's Academy for Urban Leadership; Math for America; and NYC Teaching Fellows all offer alternative certification options. Cohort three includes retirees from professions such as technology, law enforcement, business, social services, management, science and the arts.

Here is an example of the process going on to promote the idea of retired professional entering the teaching profession. Fidelity Investment, the financial service company, is running a series of ads that feature "an aging boomer in front of a classroom—graying temples, full of engagement. The message at the top: 'What did you want to do before you started doing what you are doing?'" The AARP's research indicates teaching is the number one "preferred post-midlife occupation."[2]

The alternative pathways to enter the teaching profession after retirement are growing rapidly. The Department of Defense and the Department of Education have created the Troops-To-Teachers program. The program focuses on the need to make quality teachers available for high-need schools school districts throughout America. The program offers participants stipends of $5,000 to help pay for teacher certification costs if they agree to teach for three years in a high need school district. Bonuses of $10,000 are available to participants who agree to teach for three years in a school that serves a high percentage of students from low-income families.

The Troops-To-Teachers program information page indicates that the program's goal is to pursue the aim of helping relieve the teacher shortage, especially in math, science, special education, vocational/technical and other high-needs subject areas while assisting military personnel in making successful transitions to second careers in teaching. Recipients must have a baccalaureate or advance degree and have at least ten years of service.[3]

IBM Corporation has launched a Transition to Teaching program. It began in 2005 to help address the critical shortage of math and science teachers by leveraging the brains and backgrounds of some of its most experienced employees, helping them to become fully accredited teachers in their local communities upon retiring from the company. It aid s them with certification, student teaching and subsidies. In addition to grants up to $15,000 per employee to defray the costs of schooling, IBM provides employees with up to four months of paid time to fulfill their student teaching requirement.

Stanley Litow, Vice President of IBM Corporate Citizenship & Corporate Affairs, said of the program, "People aren't ready for retirement at age 52 or 53 years old, IBM's average retirement age. These retiring employees want to continue working in positions that offer them the opportunity to give back to society in a meaningful way. Transferring their skills from IBM to the classroom is a natural for many, especially in the areas of math and science. They want the opportunity for a second career."[4]

Chicago's Academy for Urban School Leadership (AUSL) offers a $30,000 salary for one year, a $5,350 Americorp Education Award, discounted tuition at National-Louis University and financial aid loans and grants eligible for forgiveness through post-program teaching in a high-needs school. Residents of the program commit to teaching for four years following a one-year training program in a high-needs Chicago public school. Ninety percent of Class of 2010 program graduates are now employed as teachers in AUSL-managed schools.[5]

Math for America (MfA), with its focus on New York City high school math teachers, is a highly selective five-year program in which recent college graduates and mid-career professionals make a commitment to teach mathematics in public secondary schools. The fellowship includes a regular teaching salary over four years, $100,000 in stipends, full tuition for one year earning a master's degree in education or alternative credentials, and participation in MfA corps activities and professional development.[6]

The NYC Teaching Fellows program is designed specifically to provide fellows with the training, support and resources needed to succeed as a teacher in New York City public schools. The NC Teaching Fellows web page suggests, "Teaching Fellows are ready to make a difference in the lives of their students starting on the first day in front of the classroom." All NYC Teaching Fellows complete an intensive preservice program including a hands-on teaching experience in a city classroom. Fellows develop the skills needed to be successful through a subsidized master's degree program and teach full time while earning the degree at a partnering university. Upon entering the classroom as a full-time teacher, they are certified to teach in New York City under the "Transitional B Certification."

Once fellows secure a full-time position, they receive the same salary and benefits as other beginning teachers. First-year teacher salary in New York City in 2010 was $45,530. Fellows are recent college graduates and a diverse group of professionals seeking a career transition to teaching.[7]

Clearly teachers from alternative certification programs are needed to shore up the teaching profession that is experiencing the record exit of both novice and veteran teachers. But there can be a hidden cost for teachers when their school districts sign contracts with these alternative certification programs to employ their corps members as beginning teachers. When school budgets face tough economic times, teachers, even successful mid-career teachers, can be laid off and replaced by novice teachers from these contracted programs.

They can be displaced because the contracts agreed to by the school districts require a fixed number of corps teachers to be employed no matter what local issues arise. Budget problems or not, they stay. Hometown, homegrown, reliable teachers with star evaluations can be laid off and replaced by novices arriving from faraway places, not a good mix either for the new arrivals or those teachers already employed by the school district.

While buyouts of veteran teachers are causing a brain drain or our most successful vet teachers, new alliances between alternative certifications programs and school districts can have even a worse scenario. These alliances have the potential to lead to the laying off of teachers without a buyout, teachers who are guilty of having done nothing but work hard and become successful employees. They can be replaced by young Ivy League grads who arrive in high need schools, welcomed, acclaimed, but with no experience, untested.

Once news gets around the school about the contract requirements, the buzz among teachers is, "Watch out, these new rookies might take our jobs. We could all be on the endangered list." The teachers become like some of their at-risk students, on uneasy ground, always waiting to see if they are being called to the principal's office, wondering if their number is up.

It's not a positive situation in a high-need school, and it's not a way to boost a negative school climate. Instead, a divisive new element is being added that can quickly cause a schism between the old and the new. It's not an environment that encourages mid-career and veteran teachers to mentor and support the newcomers. Rather, it's an environment in which the key words are "watch your back."

As researchers Carole Edelsky and Jenise Porter report, the hiring of Teach for America (TFA) corps teachers is seen as a money-saver for cash-strapped districts. TFA teachers can be hired at the lowest pay. Many districts contract with the organization to hire its recruits while at the same time laying off veteran teachers.[8]

In response to a defense of TFA, the *Queens Teacher* blogger writes, "What make TFA wrong is that it encourages high turnover in staff. A school staffed with new teachers year after year is a WEAK school. Say what you want about veteran teachers, but the fact of the matter is that they are an asset to the school. Are there duds out there? Sure. That can be said for most professions. Would you want your kids to be taught by brand new teachers every year? I know I wouldn't. It takes YEARS to master teaching."[9]

Veteran teachers aren't the only ones at risk when alternative certification programs and high-need school districts form an alliance. The corps teachers are at risk as well. They are often clueless when they are hired about what can go wrong for them in the real school world. Maybe they are committed, hopeful, and dedicated but they can be vulnerable and naive about life in the classroom. Some students and parents can be difficult, even cruel. They've seen inexperienced teachers come and go and some have played a part in getting rid of them.

Some colleagues can be difficult or cruel as well. These corps teachers can quickly find themselves at risk upon entering a hostile school environment where they are often unfairly stereotyped as self-serving intruders, just doing time before they move on to a better job. As some teachers say in the faculty room, "They're raw meat. They'll be chewed up by the kids. I give them six months at best. Then they'll go home and take a job on Wall Street."

Their level of risk is also heightened because their placements are often in high-needs secondary schools. The term "high-needs" sounds unthreatening to new recruits, at least until they arrive at such a school, which is often characterized by ongoing problems with discipline, student learning difficulties, high turnover of staff, little parent or community support, students involved in the court system, poor student attendance and a high dropout rate.

The corps members' learning curve in these high-needs schools, where there may be a low level of morale among staff who are deeply sensitive to losing their jobs, may be too steep for some. It may be a major cause for their exit after the required two-year involvement comes to an end, or sooner, much sooner. Even if they become star teachers they leave before they master their craft.

Chris Turk, A Teach for America corps member teaching middle school social studies at Cherry Hill Elementary/Middle School in Baltimore, suggests, "I think there's no level of training you can receive, whether it's Teach for America or any other nonprofit organization, that's going to adequately prepare you for a low-income school system." Turk also says the charge that TfAers perpetuate chronic turnover in low-income schools is a "fair criticism."[10]

Some of these dynamics surface in reviews and observations about the Teach for America (TFA) program. And it is TFA that is drawing the most criticism from veteran teachers and teacher unions. The goal of Teach for America is to provide a critical source of well-trained teachers who can break the cycle of education inequity. Teachers, called corps members, commit to teach for two years in one of thirty-nine urban and rural regions across the country, going above and beyond traditional expectations to help their students to achieve at high levels. Teach for America's 20,000 alumni are playing critical leadership roles in the effort to improve the quality of public education in low-income communities.

Teach for America corps members receive a full salary plus comprehensive health and retirement benefits. Salaries range from $30,000 to $51,000, depending on the region. They are fully employed by a school district and receive the same salaries and benefits of other beginning teachers. Health benefits and full retirement benefits are supplied by the school district and usually include employer-supported pension plans and 401(b) investment accounts.

Teach for America recently received a fifty-million-dollar "scale-up" grant, to be paid over four years, through the U.S. Department of Education's Investing in Education Innovation (i3) competition. Five other organizations founded or run by Teach for America—KIPP, the New Teacher Project, New Schools New Orleans, IDEA Public Schools and the School for One—also won i3 grants.[11]

But questions abound about the effectiveness, favoritism, and special treatment of the Teach for America Program. Maybe the criticism is unfair, unwarranted, or unsubstantiated but it is there, the elephant in the room amid all the hype for TFA. For example, Greg Toppo raises the question of whether the program is costing experienced teachers their jobs. In his article for *USA Today*, Toppo reports that Teach for America has grown steadily in recent years despite the recession and state budget crises. But it is starting to get some flak from critics who say it is forcing more experienced teachers out of their jobs.

Toppo reports that Boston Teachers Union President Richard Stutman said that TFA members replaced twenty pink-slipped teachers. Stutman said, "These are people who have been trained, who are experienced and who have good evaluations, and are being replaced by brand-new employees." Stutman said he met with eighteen other local union presidents recently and that all of them reported seeing teachers laid off to accommodate TFA hires, who enter the classroom at beginner's salary level with TFA-underwritten training.

In March of 2010, Peter Gorman, superintendent of Charlotte-Mecklenburg Schools in North Carolina, laid off hundreds of teachers but spared one hundred TFA teachers because the district had "made a commitment to the program."

TFA responded that it's a "mistaken notion" that corps members are replacing older teachers. However, John Wilson, executive director of the

National Education Association, the country's largest teacher union, takes the same position as both Stutman and Gorman. In a May 2008 memo, Wilson said that union leaders were beginning to see districts lay off teachers and then hire TFA members because of the contracts the school systems had signed. He contends that TFA hurts children by putting the "least prepared" and "least experienced" in their classrooms.

Detroit Teachers' Union President Keith Johnson also put it bluntly last April, 2010, calling TFA teachers "educational mercenaries" who "ride in on their white horses and for two years share the virtues of their knowledge as a pit stop on their way to becoming corporate executives."

Toppo adds that only 4 percent of TFAers go into business. But only 29 percent of alumni are still in the classroom. About two-thirds remain in education, mostly administrative jobs or working with policy or charitable groups.[12]

Alternative certification programs have become a needed and necessary part of the teacher preparation landscape but they are not without problems and questionable practices. The problem is not so much with their mission to fill our classrooms with well-trained, dedicated teachers; that's a good thing. But in some cases they promise more than they can deliver.

For example, they send a subtle message to teachers in high-needs schools that they are not up to the job of raising the achievement levels of students and that what is needed is an infusion of alternative certification teachers who are specially prepared for this task. This creates a hostile environment and reception for the corps teachers, a process that can leave them isolated and unsupported at the very time they need mentoring and support to survive.

Remember TFA teacher Chris Turk's comment, "I think that there is no level of training you can receive, whether it's Teach for America or any nonprofit corporation, that's going to adequately prepare you for a low-income public school system."[13]

The aggressive marketing and selling of alternative certification programs to gain a foothold in the public schools can overreach and have too much self-serving hype. The marketing strategy portrays corps teachers as the best and brightest teachers and as saviors of the students, parents, and school districts. What is missing in this strategy is any mention of the difficult challenge these corps teachers will face and the hard truth that they will need support from school staff to find their way.

Simply put, they can't survive or make a dent in raising student achievement on their own. Less hubris, a little humility, and some praise for teachers working on the front lines of high-needs schools would go a long way in making new friends and colleagues and leave their corps teachers at less risk of failure.

New York Times reporter Michael Winerip says Teach for America offers a carefully crafted elite brand name that is convincing graduates of the top undergraduate schools, including Harvard, Yale, Dartmouth, Duke, Georgetown, and the University of North Caroline at Chapel Hill, to come on board. TFA is a brand name that can help build a resume, whether or not the person stays in teaching. And in a bad economy it's a two-year job guarantee with a good paycheck.[14]

These elite brand names are convincing school boards that their programs are a great deal. A major point in this marketing strategy is selling school boards that they will be getting grads of Ivy League and other top colleges and universities as teachers in their communities, bringing with them the best research and methodology that money can buy. They emphasize that the school district will become a part of a major nationwide school reform network. Extra cost is not a factor as corps teachers will be making the same salaries as any beginning teachers.

Joining the programs ensures that their schools and communities are going to be stars on the national education scene, just what is needed to turn their schools around and rebuild the public support that they have been losing.

The school district won't have to go through the problems of late hiring of new teachers when candidates withdraw their applications and opt to sign on with more affluent districts. Late hires often have little time to prepare before school starts. TFA corps teachers are signed early and are ready to go.

And finally, as TFA data suggest, they will be getting teachers from the 4,500 selected out of 46,359 applicants in 2009, the best.[15]

For hardworking teachers serving on the front lines in high-needs schools, a careful reading of the Teach for America approach on their website suggests otherwise. The TFA approach is described this way: "These teachers go above and beyond traditional expectations to help their students achieve high levels."[16] It is easy for hardworking teachers in high-needs schools to translate the meaning of "traditional expectations" as a slap in their face.

They may be hearing it as a preemptive attack that implies, "You guys and gals who are now teaching in high-needs schools aren't getting the job done. You are out of date, using the same methods that have been handed down to you by colleagues from another time. Tradition is winning out. We are coming into our school armed with the latest and best research, methodology and practices. Let us help you to be better teachers. This savior approach lacks awareness of the possibility that maybe teachers don't want or need saving.

The alliance between school districts and alternative certification programs is helping to speed up a climate of out-with-the-old, in-with-the-new. It seemingly pits the best and brightest college grads against the teachers in the trenches. A new wave, an elite brand known nationally whose marketing strategy suggests they have all the answers, are moving in and strutting their stuff. They may be young and inexperienced but they are backed up by an organization with powerful friends and alumni in high-level educational policy and management positions, wealthy foundations, huge grants, and powerful policy makers from Washington think tanks.

Their coming on board can create a faceoff with the "little guys and gals" teaching in the trenches, many of whom are trying to do their best, perhaps longing for support and affirmation but left isolated to focus on retirement and getting out. No one is giving them reason to stay. They don't have foundation and think tank support, huge grants, friends in high places or now, with the heralded arrival of the teaching corps, even public support.

The battle has been joined between alternative certification programs and mid-career and veteran teachers in the schools. It has the appearance of young versus old, new kid on the block versus the old timers, with the old timers being given no reason to stay. It's too bad because the young need to guidance and mentoring of the old-timers and the old-timers need the excitement and vitality of the young.

How do we reverse this trend in our schools and avoid ending up with novice teachers greatly outnumbering the veteran and mid-career teachers? A school community without the wisdom of old-timers to show the way is headed for trouble.

THE SEEDS ARE BEING PLANTED FOR A SCHOOL FACULTY LARGELY COMPOSED OF NOVICE TEACHERS

The battle is joined. Retirees from many professions, teacher education graduates, and graduates from alternative certification programs such as those mentioned previously are all vying for entry-level jobs in education. There is a restless army of would-be teachers knocking at the school gate. They want in!

This waiting army can't help but respond to the growing cry of "out with the old, in with the new" when it comes to the teacher workforce. It's a path for them to land a job even if veteran teachers have to be bought out. They fail to understand that someday soon, very soon, they may need support and mentoring from these retiring teachers.

Many school boards are welcoming these groups, opening up the school gates and saying, "Come on in, we have a place for you." Meanwhile, they ignore a warning light that flashes, "These are inexperienced, untested people. Beware. Do we really want to build a school faculty around so many new teachers who have never stepped foot in a real classroom? Do we want to risk suffering a large staff turnover each year, perpetuating a cycle of always hiring low-cost, inexperienced teachers?"

It will cause havoc for the foreseeable future if the three-for-one model takes hold, successful veteran teachers out and novices in by the score. Some veteran teachers, as Boston Teachers Union President Richard Stutman and Charlotte-Mecklenburg school superintendent Peter Gorman suggest, didn't even get a buyout. Instead, because of contract commitments to Teach for America, they were laid off, replaced by brand-new TFA employees.

Imagine a condition in which all is quiet in the peaceful days of summer before school opens in September. It's the kind of eerie quiet that takes place before a hurricane strikes. The new teachers readying their classrooms, the registering of new students, students coming in for sports physicals, and custodians repainting the gym floor—all seems normal and peaceful.

Little do these new teachers, or the entire school community, know that they are about to be tested come fall, when the real world of school arrives with its bedlam, crisis, and waning control over the new, negative school climate brought about by the "out-with-the-old, in-with-the-new" approach. It's a scene that may become commonplace in our secondary schools, particularly in urban areas.

Those professionals who choose teaching as the number one preferred post-midlife occupation, as described in the AARP research, and alternative certification program corps teachers may have second thoughts about their decisions when they look for support, training, and mentors come late fall but find no one to answer their calls for help.

SAVING OUR BEST AND BRIGHTEST NEW AND OLD TEACHERS

New York Times reporter Sam Dillon suggests that the retirement of thousands of baby boomers coupled with the departure of younger teachers frustrated by the stress of working in low-performing school is fueling a crisis in teacher turnover that is costing districts a substantial amount of money as they scramble to fill their ranks for the fall term. The National Commission on Teaching and the American Future, a nonprofit group that seeks to increase the retention of quality teachers, estimates that teacher turnover is costing the nation's districts some seven billion dollars for recruiting, hiring, and training.

Dillon reports that Thomas G. Carroll, president of the National Commission on Teaching and the American Future, feels, "The problem is not mainly about retirement. Our teacher preparation system can accommodate the retirement rate. The problem is that our schools are like a bucket with hole in the bottom and we keep pouring in teachers." According to the

Commission, nearly a third of all new teachers leave the profession after three years almost half are gone in five years, a disruptive situation, especially in poor neighborhoods.[17]

Amid all this furor and negativism there is hope and new paths can be taken. After all, this is a situation we have created ourselves and it can be fixed. My vision of what can be done would necessitate joining inexperienced young novices with older skilled veteran teachers as partners, teammates, learners, and champions of each others' work and careers, forming a mutual intervention process to recapture the worth of professional lives headed out the school door.

I suggest a new model to follow. It is diametrically opposite to the three-for-one model in which high-salaried veteran teachers are bought out and replaced by two or three low-salaried novices. It is a model based on the new world of retirees who want the freedom to work. This model pays attention to our highly skilled veteran teachers, offering them a reason to stay on board in their schools and be helpful in a leadership role as mentors instead of retiring. This model asks education leaders to look within to their own skilled staff as a key resource to solve the problem of teacher retention, not look elsewhere.

It's also a model to save our novice teachers, whether they come out of traditional teacher education of alternative certification programs. We need talented teachers on board regardless of their background and training. My model would make easily accessible support and mentoring available in schools on an ongoing basis, provided by teachers who have become part of a cadre of skilled veteran teachers now serving part-time as mentors, veteran teachers who commit to staying on and giving all new teachers, no matter their background, the training and support they need to survive and then thrive.

Here is how it works. But first a little background. Jewellyn Holder, the teacher described in this story, is a graduate of the New York City Teaching Fellows program and a former hospital administrator. Employed as a third-grade teacher at PS 35 in New York City, she is fortunate to receive mentoring two days a week from veteran teacher Lori Gordon.

Holder is an example of why novice teachers need a veteran teacher nearby to serve as a mentor, teammate, and friendly shoulder to lean on. It's a case of the novice needing the wise mentor and the wise mentor needing the opportunity and challenge to guide the novice. Holder says many of the teaching fellows she sees at weekly meetings and in her graduate classes feel unsupported in their schools and jealous of the extra help she is getting.

Holder says, "I just say, 'Thank God I'm in this school.'"

New York Times reporter David M. Herszenhorn followed the teaching career of novice New York City teacher Jewellyn Holder and tells her story.

Jewellyn gave up her job in 2009 at Montefiore Medical Center in the Bronx to try her hand at teaching in the New York City public schools. To ready herself Ms. Holder enrolled in the NYC Teaching Fellows program for people who wanted to change careers.

According to Education Department statistics, the odds are against her. More than half of career-changers entering the schools quit after three years. But Ms. Holder, who teaches third grade a PS 35 on East 163rd Street in the Bronx, says her second year is even better than her first and she plans to stick it out. She says her resolve is largely due to Lori Gordon, who has taught for seven years and spends two days a week in Ms. Holder's class as a mentor.

Teachers and students at PS 35 and nine other schools in District 9 in the Bronx are part of a bold experiment that Schools Chancellor Joel I. Klein believes will reinvent how teachers are trained to do their jobs, by carving out a new role for veteran educators and paying them to fill it.

For the new teachers the goal is to improve the abysmal retention rates, which officials have reached their highest levels. For the veterans the hope is to give them a reason not to retire or to leave the city for higher paying jobs in the suburbs. . . .

The program formalizes something many principals say they have done informally for years, find someone to take over a dynamic teacher's class for a period or two so that teacher can go and be a role model for others. . . . [Chancellor Klein says that] "If you create a team, a group of master teachers, and you compensate them and give them a leadership role, it's going to pay long term dividends."

Under the program, 36 veteran teachers like Ms. Gordon are now *lead teachers* who work in pairs, sharing one class and spending the other half of their time mentoring less experience teachers. They observe lessons, dispense advice, demonstrate teaching techniques and generally offer an extra pair of hands. The job pays $10,000 above their regular salary and also requires them to attend four hours of training a month.

The stakes are significant. More than 40 percent of city teachers quit within three years and nearly half leave within five years. And studies have found that more teachers leave because they feel unsupported. But teachers and principals involved say the program offers numerous benefits . . . [such as] increased credibility because the mentors are not outside experts but veteran teachers in the same school and the program was leading to more conversation and collegiality among school staff members.

At PS 35 Ms. Gordon . . . shares a fourth grade class with Lauren Koster, a 10-year veteran and while one is teaching, the other is mentoring. . . . Graciela Navarro, the principal at PS 35, said that having the lead teachers allowed her to focus her attention elsewhere rather than worrying constantly about the newest teachers on her staff and frequently dropping in on them. "I trust Ms. Gordon and Ms. Koster," she said. I will go in there but I feel I don't have to spend an extended amount of time. It gives me the opportunity to focus on another teacher and another grade."

Chancellor Klein said that . . . "because of the extra money you can attract people," adding that the higher pay might also keep more talented veterans from leaving. Carmen Vargas who has been a city educator for 32 years, said becoming a lead teacher in PS 73 in District 9 has changed her mind about retiring, not because of the money but because of the more rewarding role.

"Being able to help these new teachers makes me feel my 32 years of experience have finally paid off," she said. "Veteran teachers, we don't want to leave the system but we want to feel we are needed."[18]

Herszenhorn writes, "Randi Weingarten, president of the New York City Teachers' Union, said the program was succeeding in District 9 largely because of community support and the strong partnership between the community, the union and the school system." But as Herszenhorn reveals that the program does have its critics. "Jill Levy, the president of the principals' union, said the lead teachers were little more than a different version of the coaches, staff developers and more traditional mentors. [She said,] "I don't believe in taking teachers out of the classroom. We already have staff developers who do that, we have coaches who do that, and we have assistant principals who do that. You don't waste time by having two teachers in one room. You are taking your best teachers and removing them from the classroom."[19]

While I don't know Ms. Levy, I can understand the reluctance of some central office and building administrators to adopting the lead teacher program. My sense is that they are guarding their territory and protecting the mentoring roles of staff developers, coaches, and assistant principals. They may be leery that programs such as lead teachers could take root and diminish traditional mentoring roles that they supervise.

After all, new roles for veteran teachers who work side by side with newcomers to improve their skills are focused on individual schools, not an entire district. They employ lead teachers who are an integral part of the school community and known for their skills and leadership abilities. They are homegrown, as the saying goes. This kind of school reform can be seen as threatening by some principals and central office staffs that see staff development as their domain, not the domain of classroom teachers, no matter how skilled at the mentoring process.

But lead teachers are different from the staff developers, coaches, and consultants, who appear infrequently at best from district offices, state education departments, and college and university schools of education. These are strangers who are not part of the school community and offer little or no long-term continuity and support. They are not around when novices need, as Lori Gordon says, a mentor, teammate and friendly shoulder to lean on.

Their role is different from Ms. Levy's observation that "we have assistant principals who do that." Lead teachers are not supervisors nor do they have any formal supervision role. Neither do they have an evaluation role that can become part of the process of retaining or firing a nontenured teacher. Rather, the role of the lead teacher is as a caring partner in helping young teachers get better at their craft. It's a one-on-one process where trust and mutual respect are key and where risk-taking in trying out new approaches is encouraged.

As Ms. Gordon implies, the role is multidimensional ranging from being a mentor, a teammate and a friend, not an administrator-supervisor.

I understand if the lead teacher role brings forth resistance from some administrators as they watch experienced veteran teachers assume a leadership role, one they might find threatening and in competition with their own supervisory role. It's threatening because it puts into play an easily accessible mentoring model that has the potential to limit the more traditional role of staff developers, coaches. and assistant principals.

Ms. Levy says, "I don't believe in taking teachers out of the classroom." This perhaps suggests that the traditional role of teacher is to teach students, remain in their classrooms, and not venture out the door and become mentors.

However, if veteran teachers do begin to divide their time between their classrooms and mentoring, some administrator's inclination might be that it's best to keep the lid on this kind of school-based mentoring to ensure the jobs of their own staff development team. Protecting our own makes sense to those in charge.

Yet Ms. Levy's comments represent a helpful and important piece in our discussion about the need for new roles for veteran teachers. The voices of building and central office administrators will have to be heard and reckoned with by educators promoting the lead teacher model. They have to be sold on any kind of reform that they perceive as taking away some of their power and staff in a suffering economy. The selling part becomes a lot easier when it's being done at the highest levels by leaders such as Chancellor Klein and union president Weingarten.

Fortunately PS 35 principal Graciela Navarro doesn't see the lead teachers as competition. Being on the front line of the program, she is able to grasp the positive benefits of the leadership role, not only for her novice teachers but for her own job. She has not become defensive, making sure the program doesn't take root. Clearly we will need more principals like Ms. Navarro if this model is to take hold in our schools.

Here are some highlights of this model that offers a win-win solution:

• Highly skilled retirement-eligible teachers are given a reason to stay and use their skills to mentor new colleagues in their home schools. Their hard-earned experience is being rewarded.

- Mentoring is offered to teachers in their home schools by veteran teachers who have taught for years. They are a known quantity, not outsiders from a university, a staff developer, or a retired teacher.
- They are given a new dual role: a part-time leadership role as a mentor and a part-time role as a teacher.
- This new role carries a stipend that demonstrates that the school district values the work and wants to compensate for it.
- Inexperienced teachers from both teacher education and alternative certification programs are given the same mentoring so they can succeed in the often traumatic first years on the job. There is no pass for prior training or graduate degrees.
- The mentoring role is shared, thus offering the two mentors needed support from each other and providing a source of new learning. They are not alone or isolated.
- This mentoring role also allows building principals needed support to use their skills and leadership roles to increase supportive contact with other teachers, support staff, parents and community members. They are not isolated and alone but have mentor colleagues available as sounding boards. Principals are often isolated and on their own.
- This new mentoring role reduces the isolation of beginning teachers, building principals, and the mentors themselves, whose skills can now be transferred to colleague as well as student.
- The program helps to reduce isolation and divisions between young and veteran teachers as well as between teachers and administrators, bringing about more collegiality among staff.

While the mentoring program has come under criticism from the principals' union, it has support, financial backing, and political cover from five key constituents: the community, teachers' union, school system, school principal, and supportive members of the school faculty. This is necessary cover when new roles such as the lead teacher are seen as challenging the traditional staff development intervention roles that have been in place for decades. Transformation efforts, even minor ones, usually bring out an army of resisters.

LESSONS LEARNED FROM THE PROGRAM TO HAVE VETERAN TEACHERS IN NEW YORK CITY SCHOOLS HELP COLLEAGUES SHARPEN THEIR SKILLS

Utilizing veteran teachers to mentor and guide novice teachers is a win-win solution. Herszenhorn's article provides a concrete example of how both novice and veteran teachers benefit. Novices such as Ms. Holder get the mentoring and support they need to make a successful transition from being an anxious rookie to being a competent teacher. Veteran teachers such as Lori Gordon and Lauren Koster get the opportunity to use their experience to mentor and support fledgling teachers like Ms. Holder.

The New York City lead teachers program is an example of how to solve a major problem facing our schools—retaining novice teachers by utilizing veteran teachers as lead teachers, giving them a reason not to retire. It's an intervention process that takes place in their home school on a weekly basis.

It is a win-win situation for the entire PS 35 school community, novice teachers, veteran teachers, administrators, students, and parents. However, in my experience as a school reformer I have found that what early on appears to be a win-win solution for reform projects founders early on because the projects lack a niche to successfully mesh with more traditional programs. In the case of the New York City lead teacher initiative, that means lead teachers having a niche that enables them to be seen as an added resource and benefit for the following points.

1. Traditional staff development, coaching and administrative intervention to support and mentor novice teachers. The concerns of education leaders who are critics of the lead teacher initiative have to be heard and they must be brought on board even if they are reluctant supporters.

Their concerns about the lead teacher intervention diminishing their own staff development efforts are real, and they need to be sold on the idea that building-based lead teachers are not a threat but rather a natural extension of their mentoring efforts that will attract favorable attention to their program. Support from members of the school and union hierarchy goes a long way to ensure support in the effort to find a niche for the lead teacher program in the school organization.

Herszenhorn reports, "Chancellor Klein is convinced of its potential benefit and that expanding it has become one of his top priorities in the late stages of contract negotiations with the union."[20] Klein's position adds a wallop to the selling process and enrolling support of critics, as does the support of teacher union president Randi Weingarten.

2. Veteran teachers may see their role as classroom teachers for students, not staff developers or mentors. Teachers are often leery and suspicious of colleagues who are seeking new roles and opportunities beyond the classroom role.

In my book *An Administrator's Guide to Better Teacher Mentoring* I provide an example of the resistance that can come from colleagues when veteran educators are given the opportunity to move beyond their regular role as classroom teacher.[21] Herszenhorn's reporting on PS 35 and lead teachers Lori Gordon and Lauren Koster's experience doesn't include this complicated, tricky element, but it needs attention, as it is a part of the pressure on skilled educators such as Gordon and Koster to make a decision: .

"Yes, I am taking this lead teacher job; I'm ready for a change, a second act. I know my role in the school will be different but I need some risks in my life." Or, "No, I decided not to give up my full-time teaching role. I've been getting a lot of negative feedback about trying to get out of the classroom and be a staff developer or administrator. Not so much to my face but to my friends. They tell me there are even rumors about my becoming too much of a star in the faculty. I don't t' want any part of being in a job where there is all this hostility toward me."

I know firsthand what can happen when one changes roles, especially when it's a new role that has never existed in the faculty—such as the lead teacher's role. Even if the role is part-time it can cause resistance from colleagues who feel jealous or angry because they feel stuck and dead-ended in their role. "Getting out" can stir up resentment from colleagues and personal fears of leaving a close group one has been aligned with and going out on one's own, leaving the security and comfort of the nest. One is left with two choices: face the fact that resentment is part of life and deal with it, or give in to the resentment and stay put, avoid being seen as "out of the club" and different.

Bear in mind that veteran educators who take on new roles will not have the support of every colleague. Finding their niche can be elusive in the beginning days and months. They may find themselves out in front on their own until there is concrete positive feedback that what they are doing does help veteran colleagues as well as novices. Positive feedback from colleagues, as Herszenhorn reports about the PS 35 mentors, offers support for the program because "the teachers involved are not outside experts but veteran teachers in the same school." Supporters also said that the program "was leading to more conversation and collegiality among school staff members."[22]

Moving on has its risks but risks are what make second acts in one's career possible. You can't get to second base with your foot still on first base.

In my case I was a counselor in a junior high school. I had recently returned to school after receiving my doctorate degree. The principal of the school and I forged an alliance with a nearby university to create a teacher training center at our school. I was asked to become director of the center and also continue my role as counselor, both part time positions. But in the beginning days of the project I discovered that finding my niche was no easy task.

Teachers with outside connections, even ones like me who have roots in the school, are often not trusted or quickly accepted by the teaching staff. One is tested anew, sometimes very aggressively, by veteran teachers who are suspicious of educators who want to use their turf, even if it involves a former colleague. I returned to Bay Shore different in the eyes of many teachers. I had a PhD, had written professional articles, and spoken at district, state, and national conferences. I had become a star teacher, a somebody.

Although I saw myself as humble, eager to help others shine their light, and definitely not self-promotional, in the eyes of many teachers, particularly the veterans, I was no longer in the club. I had moved on while they remained in the trenches, teaching the same subject in the same room for years with no hope for novelty or change. In their eyes I had escaped.

The school grapevine was active with doubts: "Why should we get behind a program to support a star who probably is going to use this experiment to move on to some big job at a university or at the department of education?

Because many teachers have little opportunity for positive affirmation, they are at risk for and vulnerable to anger and resistance to any colleague who appears to have, as one teacher described it, *made it out*. I learned first-hand that the anger and resistance to me and my idea for the center was not so much about me as a person and a professional, but were reserved for anyone who had gotten out of the sometimes stagnating daily grind of teaching.

For many veteran teachers, even though they feel trapped, the opportunity for change is also anxiety producing and risky. For example, offering teachers the opportunity to lead workshops for their peers and to be released from their classrooms for the day was frightening. Many felt uncomfortable teaching their peers. Some anticipated negative feedback and rejection. It is not easy moving from teaching kids to teaching adults who know how to tune you out. Adults can't be silenced by threats such as, "You're out of here. Go to the office."

Education reformers sometimes think they are helping veteran teachers by opening new doors to opportunities for renewal, but help is in the eye of the beholder. We need to understand that we are dealing with teachers who have never experienced a world outside their classrooms. While they may know their stuff, they don't see themselves as having something to offer their colleagues. They are not star teachers, experts, conference presenters or authors. Their first inclination when asked to be a leader is to run for cover or say, "Are you sure you have the right person? I'm just a classroom teacher."

3. Teacher union leaders are being pushed hard to weed out poorly performing teachers and save their best-performing ones as school budgets are facing draconian cuts in districts throughout America. These union leaders, such as Randi Weingarten, are looking for programs such as the lead teacher initiative to demonstrate that unions are hearing the message from disgruntled citizens to save our best teachers and they use the PS 35 story to demonstrate their resolve.

A recent poll showed that voters overwhelmingly support New York City mayor Michael Bloomberg's push to base the threatened layoff of thousands of teachers on performance rather than on the current system of seniority.[23]

The *Wall Street Journal* reports,

> The Quinnipiac University poll found that eighty-five percent of voters want to spare the best teachers regardless of how long they've been on the job. They want to end the so-called "last-in, first-out" policy that would be used if the city and school districts statewide have to resort to cutting teachers' jobs. . . . In the poll even 75 percent of households with union members support performance-based criteria. "Voters, especially voters with kids in public school, want to keep the best teachers on the job and to heck with seniority," said Maurice Carroll, director of the Quinnipiac poll. He said 64 percent of voters also support raises for teachers based on merit and about the same share want to make it easier to fire ineffective teachers.

Mayor Bloomberg said of the poll results, "The public wants us to do the right thing for their children's future. That means focusing on merit to ensure we keep the very best teachers in our schools."[23]

Union leaders are being forced to consider how to retain the very best teachers and create ways to curtail the careers of low-performing ones. Tripp Gabriel of the *New York Times* reports that Randi Weingarten, president of the American Federation of Teachers and former president of the New York City Teachers' Union, "urges dismissal overhaul." Weingarten announced a plan "that would give tenured teachers who are rated unsatisfactory by their principals a maximum of one school year to improve. If they did not improve, they would be fired within 100 days." Gabriel reports that

> teacher evaluations, long an obscure detail in an educator's career, have moved front and center as school systems try to identify which teachers are best at improving student achievement and to remove ineffective ones. The issue has erupted recently with many districts anticipating layoffs because of slashed budgets. Mayors, including Michael Bloomberg of New York City and Cory A. Booker of Newark, have attacked seniority rules, which require teacher dismissals be based on length of experience rather than competency. . . . Kati Haycock, president of the Education Trust, which seeks to narrow the achievement gap for poor students partly by raising teacher quality, says, "The overall proposal is a big step forward."
>
> Ms. Weingarten [argues] that if a national evaluation process were in place, ineffective teachers would be weeded out naturally."All these folks now really concerned about layoffs for newer teachers never spent a minutes talking about how to keep good teachers in our profession," she said.[24]

There is a niche being created right now for union leaders to support new roles such as lead teacher for veteran teachers. Many school districts are anticipating huge layoffs because of slashed budgets. Meanwhile, politicians, teachers' union leaders, and school boards are jockeying to find agreement on the best way to retrain our best teachers and get rid of ineffective ones, a political process that could take years. Unions can use the lead teacher model to argue that they hear the call to keep our best teachers on board and are taking action.

Here are some examples of the fight and delays ahead on the teacher evaluation front.

• Richard Iannuzzi, president of the statewide New York Teachers United teacher union, agreed that performance should be part of the equation. But he said a system created in law last year "won't be ready for any imminent layoffs."
• Michael Mulgrew, president of the United Federation of Teachers, said that although eh seniority-based layoff policy is flawed, "it's better than letting politics take over the process."
• Michael J. Petrilli, vice-president of the Thomas B. Fordham Institute, said Weingarten's proposal did not address the most pressing issue, "how to lay off thousands of teachers because of budget cuts without losing promising newer teachers."[25]

Teacher evaluations have moved front and center to identify which teachers are best at improving student achievement and to remove ineffective ones. But solutions to the problem are not coming soon. Meanwhile, creating new roles for veteran teachers to help novices may be one doable intervention as negotiations continue among all the players in the teacher evaluation issue.

The lead teacher program offers a win-win model for teacher unions that can be part of negotiations with school districts. It's a process that speaks to the issue of how best to use the experience and skills of our veteran teachers, sparing them from running off to retirement. The program employs their skills to intervene as mentors as a preemptive strike to keep our most promising teachers on board, sparing them from failure and a fast exit. It's a process that involves identifying our best teachers to serve the newly created role as both classroom teacher and mentor for colleagues, providing skilled mentors with the reason to stay along with a financial benefit and ongoing training. It's a preemptive strike to retain our best and brightest young and old teachers.

Admittedly it's an approach that is a very small piece of the discussion of how to retain our best teachers and save our most promising younger ones. But it is a positive and inexpensive approach that enables school districts, teacher unions, policy makers and politicians to find common ground. It's a signal that they are indeed hard at work to keep our best experienced teachers and are in this fight together. Whether that is true or not, here is a way to find at least one positive intervention. It's a one-for-three "keeper" opportunity, saving one experienced teacher from retiring to mentor three or more newcomers. It's better than the wasteful three-for-one model.

4. School boards and citizen groups are calling for an "out with the old, in with the new" approach to help solve their budget problems, using the three-for-one buyouts of high-salaried staff and hiring two or three novice teachers for the same price, many from nontraditional alternative teacher education programs. While finding a positive niche to save our best teachers may be extremely difficult in this hostile environment, selling and promoting the lead teacher model as a more efficient, less divisive and less threatening approach may have support among some pro-education citizens and parents who are tired of having their children and grandchildren have a different teacher each school year.

People who care about providing a safe and positive school climate do get tired of hearing a continuous diet of bad news from their school boards regarding staff layoffs and cuts. They are looking for some good news and concrete efforts to make their schools better and keep the best and brightest teachers. They are listening and open to new paths that go beyond the anger and divisions now so common in our school district budget battles.

Buyout incentives for veteran teachers usually mean a quick financial fix followed by second thoughts when veterans are replaced by novices or substitute teachers or if their positions are left unfilled because of a teacher shortage. The situation is amplified by an effort in many states to get rid of competitive bargaining for public sector employees, including teachers, an effort that also includes replacing the seniority system that allows the layoff of last-in, first-out teachers in tough economic times and the dismantling of tenure.

The voices from ground zero in the school budget battle are telling us in many cases to find creative ways, to go back to the drawing board, to stop the brain drain of skilled veteran teachers and keep them in our schools as teachers, mentors, and leaders, to create an experienced and tested corps to guide our schools through these tough and unstable economic times. Such a leadership corps is desperately needed, as more building principals are choosing to retire or simply walk away from their high-pressure jobs.

Pat Kossan, a writer for the *Arizona Republic*, reports that some Arizona school districts are paying teachers to retire early or just leave. That has left hundreds of students in classrooms with substitutes and less experienced teachers. In some districts teachers are juggling extra classes until a permanent teacher can be found. The motivation is cost savings. Over the past five years, districts have saved millions of dollars by replacing higher-paid experience teachers with lower-paid ones. . . .

Critics say it . . . hurts student learning. Kids who have substitute or beginning teachers are at risk of falling behind in the quickening pace of education, where schools must bring more students to grade level or face a failing label. The buyouts perplex some educators. In fast-growing Arizona many schools have more openings than candidates, and educators wring their hands about baby boomers retiring early. Younger teachers are moving out of the field for better pay.[26]

The fast-growing Deer Valley Unified School Districts shed 180 teachers during a two-year buyout in the early 2000's. Now Associate Superintendent Chuck Hoover wishes he had them back. Hoover said, "We probably lost some good teachers along the way." Arizona State Retirement System officials say at least twenty-eight state school districts offer early retirement incentives but that the number may be much higher. Teachers can retire at fifty if they have taught for thirty years.

Kossan notes the downside to the buyout incentives:

The biggest risk is that school will face a brain drain. Arizona teachers' union President John Wright said pushing veteran teachers out of the classroom is a symptom of an underfunded school system. Among the schools without buyout programs are Phoenix's Isaac Elementary and Glendale Union High School districts. Mesa Public Schools dropped its early retirement program to hang on to their experienced teachers.

Glendale Union's finance administrator, Gene Dudo, said it makes no sense to buy out teachers in the middle of a teacher shortage. . . . "One could argue that a younger staff benefits a district in the long run. But you would have to consider the quality of education in the short run, and the impact would be detrimental," Dudo said.

At Scottsdale second thoughts on buyout incentives now prevail. Two weeks into the new school year, personnel chief Jeff Thomas was facing 35 unfilled teacher openings. Thomas is trying to contact some of the teachers who left during [a recent] buyout period. He wants them back. When they left, they were told that if they returned they would start at a new teacher's salary. Now, Thomas is working on a way to offer them their old salaries.[27]

Sherry Posnick-Goodwin of the California Teachers' Association, CTA) reports,

In some districts, teachers are grasping tightly when a golden handshake is extended. In others teachers have kept their distance when early retirement packages are dangled in front of them. While there are no firm numbers on how many teachers have opted to take advantage of early retirement, the trend is definitely on the rise as schools struggle with declining revenues. Even though districts have to shell out initially for the buyouts of veteran staff, districts save money over the long haul by hiring new employees with less experience for lesser salaries.

In the Los Angeles Unified School District a staggering 1,360 employees have signed up for early retirement. Under the plan teachers and counselors receive about 40 percent of their 2009–2010 salary over a period of time, along with their normal pension. The move might save some of the 3,500 position held by United Teacher Los Angeles members at risk of being laid off.

In the San Diego Unified School District nearly 600 teachers have submitted papers for early retirement under a plan that provides them with one year's salary paid out over a few years, in addition to regular retirement benefits. The district has estimated that replacing veteran teachers with lower-paid, newer teachers would save between $7.6 million and $12.3 million over the next few years.[28]

Posnick-Goodwin quotes that the reaction of San Diego Education Association to this retirement benefit is "bittersweet. The loss of veteran SDEA members is a loss to out union culture and our history."

How about the impact of their loss on students, parents, colleagues, and administrators? Posnick-Goodwin speaks to this point, saying that "some . . . fear the loss of veteran teachers may have other impacts. Experienced teachers have been counted on traditionally to provide school leadership and to mentor and support new teachers." Margaret Gaston, executive director of the Center for the Future of Teaching and Learning in Santa Cruz, adds, "In schools where there has traditionally been a lot of turnover, there has been a concern because there are not enough accomplished veteran teachers to usher novices into the profession."

Posnick-Goodwin points out that "the buyouts are happening at a time when the nation is facing the largest teacher retirement wave in history, with some 50 percent of teachers over the age of 50." In May of 2010 the National Commission on Teaching and America's Future "forecast that more than half of today's veteran teachers, 1.7 million, may be gone soon due to retirement, taking with them invaluable experience and expertise."[29]

In Harbor Spring, Michigan, Charles O'Neill of the *Harbor Light* newspaper reports that the Harbor Springs Board of Education offered early retirement to reduce the number of forced layoffs. School superintendent Mark Tompkins said, "If we are able to get five or more teachers to take this package, we could save $200,000 per year. We will not be hiring new staff. We will be doing more with the folks we have, shifting teaching responsibilities and making other adjustments."

But board president Rob Furham said, "The downside is that we lose some very experienced teachers. It's a very hard thing to do."[30]

Likewise, in Forest Hill, Michigan, Rick Wilson of the *Grand Rapids Press* reported that 121 Forest Hills teachers applied for early retirement. Wilson said, "They have seven days to reconsider." Superintendent Dan Behn said, "If we manage attrition correctly, quality will not suffer, but it takes active management." Behn estimated only about half the teachers lost to early retirement would be replaced and that at the elementary school level some grades might be split and some high school elective classes might not be offered as frequently. Teachers might also have to take on more classes.[31]

Sounds like Superintendent Behn's comment that "quality will not suffer" might not be quite accurate.

In Lancaster, California, Karen Maeshiro reports that

> after going to Minnesota, Canada and Spain to recruit teachers, two Antelope Valley school districts want to offer incentives to their most experienced and highest paid teachers to retire. Officials at the Antelope Valley Union High School District and Palmdale School District describe the supplemental retirement plan as a "gift" to experienced teachers and a way to "impressive savings" at a time of expected budget shortfalls. . . . A supplemental employee retirement program, or SERP, . . . provides a benefit to employees with the most seniority and higher pay to retire early, thus allowing districts to retain lower-paid employees or in some cases, not replace the retiring employee.[32]

However, school officials acknowledge the potential downside of replacing veteran instructors with new teachers during a teacher shortage. Quartz Hill High School's Ira Simonds, a thirty-four-year veteran, said, "The idea is, of course, they can get two teachers for the price of one, but the problem is we are not finding those teachers. There is a teacher shortage and the Antelope Valley certainly does not rank as the No. 1 spot for young people to move to. This could mean a bigger shortage." He adds, "We are still vital. The new teachers do turn to us. They don't treat us as has-beens. We do keep up. We do go to conferences. We know all the new stuff."[33]

Josh Night, a reporter for WHSV, reports on the Shenandoah County Public Schools' early retirement incentive program. He quotes Gina Stetter, a middle school principal who worries, that although the program could alleviate strain on the current budget, it will hurt to lose veteran teachers. Stetter said, "It's not just the impact they have on students in the classroom. It's the mentoring they provide to the new teachers who come in."

Andrew Ansoorian, the Shenandoah Public Schools Director of Human Resources, says, "A lot of these positions are not going to be replaced." Stetter notes that even if positions are filled again, "those years and years of experience, of being able to look at a content problem and assess, 'What should we really do for this student to make sure that he learns?' That simply can't be replaced without year and years of experience."[34]

Educators 4 Excellence (E4E), a nonprofit organization of reform-minded teachers presented in February of 2011 a comprehensive alternative to New York City's layoff policy. Under current policy teachers with the least amount of experience would be automatically laid off, regardless of their classroom skills. E4E wants classroom skills to play a leading role in determining layoffs in order to keep more great teachers in the classrooms.

Sydney Morris of E4E said, "Given that teacher effectiveness is the most important in-school factor in helping students succeed, we need to make sure that if layoffs become necessary, we keep our best teachers for students."[35]

On February 27, 2011, it was announced that 4,675 layoffs are possible as part of Mayor Bloomberg's campaign to change teacher seniority rules. City Department of Education spokeswoman Natalie Ravitz said, "The seniority system hurts school children. There is a better way to do this. We can change the law and keep the best teachers for our kids."[36]

On March 1 the New York State Assembly passed a bill that would end the seniority-based teacher layoff law for New York City Schools. The New York City teachers' union criticized the measure as "union-busting" and meant to allow Mayor Bloomberg to fire the best-paid teachers.

Paul Casciano, superintendent of the William Floyd District on Long Island, said, "My concern is that this legislation is a camouflage for eliminating more senior teachers because they cost more. At William Floyd, as our teachers get more experience, they get better."[37]

The *Arizona Republic* reports that

> In order to cut costs and lessen potential layoffs, the Peoria Unified School District plans to offer retirement incentives to more than one hundred teachers and staff. . . . Rob Contrara, a social studies teacher at Ironwood High School, is one of them. He is 52 years old with 26 years of teaching in the district, the last 19 at Ironwood. . . . Before he knew about the retirement plan, he planned on teaching 10 more years. "If it was under normal circumstances I would continue teaching," he said. Why retire? I enjoy teaching and being around kids." But with the potential changes in mind, he saw it in his best interest to retire. . . . "The best years are behind me—for me to stay would mean losing money." He said maybe a year after retiring, he will try to get hired at another school district and keep teaching.[32]

In Monon, Indiana, the North White school board accepted the retirement of nine teachers in a contract buyout offered to reduce budget woes. North White Superintendent Nicholas Eccles said, "A lot of them have committed a long time to North White. A lot of them bleed blue and white and gold and I'm very happy for them that they're willing to take the next step."[39]

Matt Miller of the *Washington Post* suggests that the best advice concerning the imminent layoff of 275,000 of the nation's roughly three million teachers is to "think 'buyout,' not 'bailout.'" Miller says,

> the coming teacher firings are doubly disastrous because labor contracts and state laws require that most layoffs be done on the basis of seniority, that is, newer teachers get the ax first. The trouble with this last-in, first-out rule is that layoffs are made with no concern for whether the teachers in question are any good. Yet in many big districts, huge efforts have been made in recent years to hire talented young teachers . . . to work with our neediest children. With one awful stroke, these layoffs could eviscerate years of such recruiting, giving poor kids the shaft once again.[40]

In Fort Collins, Colorado, "with a projected $12 million budget to make up by June [2010], the Poudre District leaders offered a buyout . . . to teachers with at least 20 years of experience in the district. . . . The result: younger, lower paid teachers will replace them." This buyout of experienced teachers did not sit well with some parents. Wendi Beld, mother of four middle school students in the district, said, "I guess I would ask them to go back to the drawing board and figure out other ways to do it. As a parent I'd probably be more willing to pay an additional $20 to a specific school if that would help."[41]

In Detroit, Wayne State University College of Education dean Paula Wood voiced a theme being offered by many colleges of education when she said a Michigan Education Association plan to get teachers to retire through a buyout would help new teachers to stay in Michigan. She said, "I just met with a large group of personnel officers and assistant superintendents and they've had very few retirements." Both traditional and nontraditional teacher preparation programs are major players in the push for veteran teachers to retire. It means more jobs for their graduates.[42]

Elsewhere in Michigan, the *Grand Rapids Press* reports, "A high number of experienced public school teachers are retiring this summer [2010], taking advantage of buyouts offered in local districts that must cut salary costs. . . . But buyouts have downsides. . . . They can be shortsighted approaches to savings and they cannot ensure that ineffective teachers are the ones who leave. More significantly, they drain school of veteran talent. 'You always lose something when people leave. You can't replace thirty years of experience in the classroom,' said Superintendent Mike Paskewicz of Northview School District." Jerry Aquino, a high school special education teacher in the Caledonia School District, said "the decision to retire was agonizing."

He said, "I don't have words to describe how it's going to be, walking out of here. Working with young people keeps you young. I'm going to miss the kids and staff terribly." Caledonia school superintendent Jerry Phillips said, "Exceptionally talented teachers like Jerry really wrestle with this decision. Teaching is such a part of them. They've made a difference for a long time."[43]

Nick Anderson of the *Washington Post* adds a new dynamic to the conversation of how best to retain our most skilled veteran teachers, reporting that "the Republican faceoff with labor unions in the Midwest and elsewhere marks not just a fight over money and collective bargaining but also a test of will over how to improve the nation's schools."

Various GOP proposals to "limit teacher bargaining rights, dismantle teacher tenure and channel public money toward private schools" raise a question. Should states work with teacher unions to overhaul education or try to roll over them? Anderson quotes Richard W. Hurd, a labor relations expert at Cornell University, who said, "If you have someone who's proposing to do away with bargaining rights, a line has to be drawn in the sand. In an environment like that it creates incredible tensions. Teachers are going to be very suspicious."

Last month the Indiana Senate passed a bill to "connect teacher evaluations with test scores, launch a system of performance-based pay, and make it easier to dismiss teachers repeatedly rated ineffective or in need of improvement." Senate Democrats are objecting to the Republican bills and some have fled the state.

Anderson says, "The statehouse battle perplexes teachers at Shortridge High School, alma mater of U.S. Senator Richard Lugar (R-Ind) and the late author Kurt Vonnegut, Jr. The theme of the 600-student magnet school is law and public policy. Arlene Smith, . . . a social studies teacher and union representative, said veteran teachers must be shielded from arbitrary firing. She said it would be a 'little frightening' if union rights are stripped. 'I'm old. I'm expensive. You could hire two people out of college for what you pay me.'"[44]

Cornell's Richard W. Hurd is right on when he suggests the current battle over bargaining rights is creating incredible tension and teachers are going to be very suspicious. Teachers have become fair game, targets in the blame game of who is responsible for the current budget shortfalls in our schools. And it's not only the veteran teachers who are being asked to accept buyouts so that districts can hire younger, inexperienced teachers. The current scorn aimed at teachers is reaching across all age groups—novices, mid-career, and veterans.

In the *New York Times*, Tripp Gabriel spells out this rising anger toward teachers: "Around the country many teachers see demands to cut their income, benefits and say in how schools are run through collective bargaining as attacks not just on their livelihood but on their value to society. Even in a country that is of two minds about teachers—Americans glowingly recall the ones who changed their lives but think the job with its summers off is cushy—education experts say teachers have rarely been the targets of such scorn from politicians and voters."

Gabriel gives as examples of this scorn Governor Chris Christie of New Jersey accusing teachers of greed and mayors threatening mass layoffs, as in Providence, RI, "where all 1,926 teachers were told in February of 2011 they would lose their jobs—a largely symbolic gesture since most would be hired back." Given this hostile environment "some experts question whether teaching, with it already high attrition rate—more than 25 percent leave in the first three years—will attract high quality recruits in the future."

Gabriel gives some teacher reactions to the hostility. Steve Derion, who teaches American history in Manahawkin, New Jersey, says, "It's hard to feel good about yourself when your governor and other people are telling you you're doing a lousy job. I am sure there were worse times to be a teacher in our history, I know they had little rights, but it feels like we're going back toward that direction."

Lindsay Vlachakis, a high school math teacher in Madison, said, "I put my heart and soul into teaching. When people attack teachers, they're attacking me."

Anthony Cody writes a blog about teaching. He taught middle-school science for eighteen years and now mentors new teachers in the Oakland, California, school district. It's a district that has many poor students at the bottom level of standardized tests. Cody says, "What we need in these schools is stability. We need to convince people that if they invest their career in working with these challenging students, then we will reward them and appreciate them. We will not subject them to arbitrary humiliation in the newspaper. We will not require that they be evaluated and paid based on test scores that often fluctuate greatly beyond the teacher's control."[45]

Cody's assessment that what we need in our schools today is stability is on the money. Stability can serve to quiet some of the antiteacher rancor sweeping the country and instead refocus our energy and creativity on ways to raise performance without spending a lot of money. In order to reach that goal we need to find ways to move many of our citizens and politicians beyond viewing teachers as their favorite punching bag in these tough economic times. We must stop devaluing the careers of successful veteran teachers by pushing them to take early buyouts, not giving them a reason and reward to stay on as mentors and advisors, or even worse, threatening them with loss of tenure if they remain in their schools.

As Cody says, we need to reward and appreciate them, not discard them as if their years of hard work had no impact or meaning. And again as Cody suggests, we must do the same for our novice and mid-career teachers, forming a school community in which teachers feel they belong and are needed, led by educators who know how to affirm and nourish each other in our increasingly battle-torn schools.

It all comes down to changing the way we use our human capital in the schools. Discarding our most successful, experienced teachers through buy-outs doesn't make sense. It's a waste of our most precious human capital. They are needed to educate, train, build up, and support novices and mid-career teachers. We need to "flip the curve" and be more aggressive, union and school leaders alike, at urging the ineffective teachers to take the buyouts, those who showed up at their school with little human capital to share or who wasted it by settling for less.

Bill Gates reminds us that while it's reasonable to suppose teachers who have served longer are more effective, the evidence says that's not necessarily true. After the first few years seniority seems to have no effect on student achievement. Gates, the co-chair of the Bill and Melinda Gates Foundation, says in a *Washington Post* article,

> To build a dynamic 21st-century economy and offer every American a high-quality education, we need to flip the curve. For more than 30 years, spending has risen while performance has stayed relatively flat. Now we need to raise performance without spending a lot more. When you need more achievement for less money, you have to change the way you spend. . . . We know that of all the variables under a school's control, the single most decisive factor in student achievement is excellent teaching. It is astonishing what great teachers can do. . . . To flip the curve we have to identify great teachers, find out what makes them so effective and transfer those skills to others so more students can enjoy top teachers and high achievement. . . . America has spent more and achieved less. If there's any good news in that, it's that we've had a chance to see what works and what doesn't. That sets the stage for a big change to help every teacher get better.[46]

In order to grow great teachers we will need both skilled veteran teachers serving as mentors and skilled building principals such as Graciela Navarro of New York City's PS 35 to guide and protect their pioneering efforts. But in the "new normal: of school life, many experienced principals and assistants are exiting their jobs because of retirement, "job hopping" instead of staying in a school district, or simply walking away because their roles have become too high-pressured. The mass exiting of veteran teachers coupled with the exiting of the school administrators is producing a double whammy. It is leaving a leadership vacuum, a vacuum that can leave our schools leaderless or guided by inexperienced and untested educators. This scenario is rapidly becoming the "new normal" in our schools, particularly our secondary schools, with a high rate of staff and administrative turnover. It's not an environment suited to growing the great teachers Bill Gates is calling for.

In Fairfield County, Connecticut's urban school districts there is a growing concern that not enough qualified school leaders are available to replace the many principals who are nearing retirement. Eight of the ten principals and assistant principals in Bridgeport's public schools will be eligible to retire within the next five years, and in Norwalk, Danbury, and Stamford, the same is true for nearly half of the school leaders.

The *New York Times* quotes Richard W. Lemons, an assistant professor at the University of Connecticut Neag School of Education: "We've been discussing a principal shortage in Connecticut and nationwide for over a decade now. The percentage of good candidates has decreased. Where we used to have ten qualified people for a job, we now have five. There are fewer names in the pot."

Dr. Lemons says one reason for the impending shortage is baby boomers are retiring in large numbers. At the same time, he says, young educators tend to "job hop" instead of advancing into leadership roles and that teachers are also leaving at mid-career, causing a further shortage of experienced candidates.

John J. Ramos, superintendent of Bridgeport Public Schools, says, "Many teachers ask, 'Is it worth it?' They look at the enormity of the workload and the financial reality of how much more they might make. For many teachers, it just isn't worth it."

Resent research by the Connecticut Center for School Change found that "principals are the most important factor in teacher retention." Dr. Ramos says, "Without an effective principal, you risk the stability of the school."[47]

Gary Gordon of the Gallup Polls Education Division says "

> Great principals naturally foster great workplaces and great workplaces encourage teachers to stay. Great principals set a tone that is likely to boost employee engagement—the degree to which employees are fully involved in and enthusiastic about their work—among teachers. . . . Great principals are able to demonstrate to teachers that they truly care about them, in both subtle and overt ways. When teachers feel cared about, they have more emotional commitment to their managers and their work. Engaged employees are more likely to go above and beyond for their managers.[48]

Gordon also writes, "The most important challenge facing our schools today is their flagging ability to recruit and retain effective teachers. Nationally, the turnover rate for beginning is 40 to 50 percent. As a result, for every

10 beginning teachers hired this year, researchers predict 4r to 5 will leave teaching."[49]

Young, inexperienced novice teachers, such as PS 25's Jewellyn Holder, need great teachers and mentors such as Lori Gordon and Lauren Koster. And they also need great principals like Graciela Navarro. Together they form a mutually supportive and trusted team working as equals to train and support the Ms. Holders of the world.

But what happens in the real school world when great teachers and mentors, along with great principals, abruptly leave their leadership positions because of buyouts or more importantly, because they are given no reason or incentive to stay on?

A 2009 study at the University of Texas Austin College of Education found that 70 percent of new high school principals leave within five years and that "principal retention matters because teacher retention and qualifications are greater in schools where principals stay longer. Any school reform efforts are reliant on the principal's creating a common school vision and staying in place to implement [it]." The study also found that "elementary schools have the longest principal tenure and greatest retention rates," and "principal retention is somewhat higher in suburban school districts where most students are white and not economically disadvantaged.

Most of the principals who leave a school actually leave principalship altogether, about 90 percent. That's a massive number. This means we have a constantly revolving door of new principals who have not had the opportunity to hone their skills and become experts at school leadership. This simply makes turnover even more likely, thus creating a vicious cycle of turnover and inexperience.[50]

The mass exodus of skilled veteran teachers and principals creates a vacuum in which inexperienced novice teachers and new principals who have not had the opportunity to hone their skills are being hired in the "out-with-the-old, in-with-the-new," new normal of school life. This creates a school environment in which the entire school community is at risk to failure—students, teachers and principals—particularly at the secondary level in high poverty areas. There results a cycle of students failing and dropping out, novice teachers failing and dropping out and new principals failing and dropping out, leaving a school with a legacy opposite to what Gary Gordon and Bill Gates hoped for—great teachers, great principals, and high-achieving students.

Chapter 6 is about ways to create new mentoring and staff development roles for great veteran teachers, roles that can enable them, as in PS 35, to transfer those skills to other teachers in an attractive, trusting and easily accessible way. While a major emphasis of this book is on retaining our best and brightest veteran teachers and intervening to help retain our best and brightest novice teachers, helping them to eventually become great teachers, there is more to this story.

These roles also serve to provide support for principals, particularly new ones, who are often isolated, under great pressure, and lacking the opportunity to hone their skills and become experts at school leadership. PS 35 mentors Lori Gordon and Lauren Koster are a team working in concert with Principal Graciela Navarro. They watch each others' backs, support each other and need each other to successfully navigate through the crises and political minefields common in our schools. They are in it together, teammates in the battle to retain novice teachers and increase student achievement. Each member of the team plays an important role.

Randi Weingarten understood this model of team intervention for novice teachers and students when describing parent and community support for the lead teacher initiative at PS 35. She said, "The community knew they needed intensive professional development that was organic, that was embedded in classrooms. That's why they wanted people in schools all the time who knew the school and also were rolling up their sleeves and teaching, not telling teachers what to do but working with teachers side by side."[51]

Thank you, Ms. Weingarten, for giving us a real picture of how the transfer of skills can take place in a real school setting, teacher to teacher and principal to teacher, creating a process and environment in which students are encouraged to transfer their newly learned skills to other students. They learn also, as needed in our high-poverty and newcomer neighborhoods, how to transfer newly learned skills to parents and family members. It's an all-for-one-and-one-for-all process instead of a vicious cycle of failure for students, novice teachers and principals.

NOTES

1. Mikki Cichocki, "Teacher Retirement Incentives + Merit Pay = Hmmm," February 21, 2010, http://mikki.com/2010/03/teacher-retirement-incentives-merit-pay-hmm/ (accessed November 4, 2010).

2. Marc Freedman, "The Selling of Retirement and How We Bought It," *Washington Post*, February 6, 2005, B01.

3. Defense Activity for Non-Traditional Education Support (DANTES), "Current Status of Troops-to-Teachers," *Shift Colors* 47, no.4, http://www.public.navy.mil/bupers-npc/reference/publications/shiftcolors/Documents/Archives/2002OCTSC.pdf (accessed February 19, 2011).

4. IBM, "Transition to Teaching: IBM Launches 'Transition to Teaching' Program," *IBM Gives News*, Fall 2008, http://ibm.com/ibm/ibmgivesnews/transition_to-eaching_shtml (accessed February 21, 2001).

5. CPS Human Resources, *Academy for Urban School Leadership (AUSL): Turning Around Schools* (Chicago, IL: Chicago Public Schools Department of Human Resources, 2007).

6. Math for America, "About MfA Fellows," 2008, http://mathforamerica.org/web/guest/about-us (accessed February 12, 2011).

7. NYC Teaching Fellows, "Overview of NYC Teaching Fellows," 2010, http://nycteachingfellows.org/program/overview.asp (accessed February 24, 2011).

8. Carole Edelsky and Jenise Porter, "Teach for America: A Bad Deal for Public Education," *Queens Teacher*, August 16, 2010, http://queensteacher2.blogspot.com/2010/08/teach-for-america-bad-deal-for-public.html (accessed October 15, 2010).

9. *Queens Teacher*, August 16, 2010, http://queensteacher2.blogspot.com/2010/08/teach-for-america-bad-deal-for-public.html (accessed October 15, 2010).

10. Gregg Toppo, "Teach for America: Elite Corps or Costing Older Teachers Jobs?" *USA Today*, July 29, 2009, http://www.usatoday.com/news/education/2009-07-29-teach-for-america_N.htm (accessed October 15, 2010).

11. Teach for America, "How We Are Helping to Solve Educational Inequality," http://www.teachforamerica.org/what-we/do/our/approach (accessed February 20, 2011).

12. Toppo, "Teach for America."

13. Toppo, "Teach for America."

14. Michael Winerip, "A Chosen Few Are Teaching for America," *New York Times*, July 11, 2010, http://www.nytimes.com/2010/07/12/education/12winerip.html?.=&adxnnl=1&ref=teach_for_america&adxnnlx=1311778150-SoFuF84e RwtrAdIFQI2dIw (accessed October 16, 2010).

15. Teach for America, "How We Are Helping."

16. Teach for America, How We Are Helping."

17. Sam Dillon, "With Turnovers High, Schools Fight for Teachers," *New York Times*, August 27, 2007, http://www.nytimes.com/2007/08/27/education/27teacher.html?sq=teacher.retention&st (accessed November 12, 2010).

18. David M. Herszenhorn, "Veteran Teachers in City Schools Help Colleagues Sharpen Skills," *New York Times*, November 1, 2004, accessed November 12, 2010, http://nytimes.com/2004/11/01/education/01teach.html/sq=teacherretention&st+cs.

19. Herszenhorn, "Veteran Teachers."

20. Herszenhorn, "Veteran Teachers."

21. William L. Fibkins, *An Administrator's Guide to Better Teacher Mentoring*, 2nd ed. (Lanham, MD: Rowman & Littlefield Education, 2011), 181, 182, 183.

22. Herszenhorn, "Veteran Teachers."

23. Michael Gormley, "Poll: NYers Want Best Teachers Spared Layoffs," *Wall Street Journal*, February 24, 2011, http://www.wsj.com/article/AP2978a33501113419f8 bd4965d8beede4.html (accessed February 25, 2011).

24. Tripp Gabriel, "Leader of Teachers' Union Urges Dismissal Overhaul," *New York Times*, February 25, 2011, A29.

25. Gabriel, "Leader of Teachers' Union."

26. Pat Kossan, "Schools Offer Buyouts amid Teacher shortage," *The Arizona Republic*, September 2, 2006, http://www.azcentral.com/arizonarepoblic/news/articles/0902oaidoff0902.html (accessed October 12, 2010).

27. Kossan, "Schools Offer Buyouts."

28. Sherry Posnick-Goodwin, "Teacher Retirement on the Rise, *California Teacher Magazine*, June 2009, accessed February 22, 2011, http://www.cta.org/Professional-Development/Publications?Educator-June-09/0609-action.29. Posnick-Goodwin, "Teacher Retirement on the Rise."

30. Charles O'Neill, "School District to Offer Teachers Early Retirement Initiative," *Harbor Light News*, April 21, 2010, http://www.harborhightnews.com/af/php/sid=10145&current_edition-2010-04-21 (accessed November 10, 2010).

31. Rick Wilson, "121 Forest Hills Teachers, Staff Apply for Early Retirement Incentive," *Grand Rapids Press*, April 15, 2010, http://www.mlive.com/news/grand-rapids/index.ssf/2010/04/121_forest+hills-teacher_st (accessed November 10, 2010).

32. Karen Maeshiro, "Exit by Veteran Teachers? Districts Weigh Early Retirement Incentives," *The Free Library*, 2002, http://www.thefreelibrary.com/EXIT+BY+VETERAN+TEACHERS%3f+DISTRICTS+ (accessed November 10, 2010).

33. Maeshiro, "Exit by Veteran Teachers?"

34. Josh Knight, "County Schools Consider Retirement Incentives," WHSV.com, February 24, 2010, http://gray.printthis.clickability.com/pt/cpt/action=cpt&title+County+Schools+consider+Retirement+Incentives (accessed November 4, 2010).

35. Education4Excellence, "City Teachers Unveil Comprehensive Plan to Reform "Last In–First Out" Layoff Policy," http://www.educators4excellence.org/ (accessed March 1, 2011).

36. Karen Matthews, "NYC Unveils Teacher Layoff Plans," *Newsday*, March 2, 2011, A6, 7.

37. Yancey Roy, "Taking Aim at Tenure in Teacher Layoffs," *Newsday*, March 2, 2011, A 6, 7.

38. Jeffrey Javier, "Early Out for Peoria Unified Teachers," *Arizona Republic*, March 17, 2010, http://www.azcentral.com/commuity/peoria/articles/2010/03/17/20100317retirement-incentives-peoria-teachers.html (accessed November 4, 2010).

39. Scott Allen, "North White Schools Buy Out 9 Teachers to Ease Budget Woes," *Herald Journal*, March 9, 2010, http://www.indianaeconomicdigest.net/main.asp/SectionalD=31&subsectionID=244&arti (accessed October 15, 2010).

40. Matt Miller, "Buyouts, Not Bailouts, for Teachers," *Washington Post*, May 11, 2010, http://www.washingtonpost.com/wp-dyn/content/article/2010/05/12/AR2010051202659.html (accessed October 13, 2010).

41. Tyler Lopez, "Budget Cuts Open Door for Some to Retire Early," *The Denver Channel*, April 10, 2010, http://www.thedenverchannel.com/print23106933/detail.html (accessed October 13, 2010).

42. Chris Christoff and Peggy Walsh-Sarnecki, "Michigan Education Association Has Plan: Get Teachers to Retire: Better Pensions for 9,000 Sought," *Detroit Free Press*, January 28, 2009, http://istockanalyst.com/article/vewiStockNews/articleid/2988408 (accessed October 12, 2010).

43. Rick Wilson, "Teacher Buyouts Could Prove to be Too Popular for Michigan Schools," *The Grand Rapids Press*, Ma 9, 2010, http://www.mlive.com/news/grand-rapids/index.ssf/2010/05/many_area_teachers_go_for_earl.html (accessed October 12, 2010).

44. Nick Anderson, "Midwest Union Battles Highlight Debate Over Improving Schools," *Washington Post*, March 3, 2011, http://www.washingtonpost.com/wp-dyn/content/article/2011/03/2/AR2011030203014_2.html (accessed March 11, 2011).

45. Tripp Gabriel, "Teachers Wonder: Why the Scorn?" *New York Times*, March 2, 2011, http://www.nytimes.com/2011/03/03/education/03teacher.html?hp=&pagewanted=print (accessed March 3, 2011).

46. Bill Gates, "How Teacher Development Could Revolutionize Our Schools," *Washington Post*, February 28, 2011, http://washingtonpost.com/wp-dyn/cntent/article/2011/02/27/AR2011022702876.html (accessed February 28, 2011).

47. Moina Noor, "Shortage of Principals Is Feared as Wave of Retirements Looms," *New York Times*, August 3, 2008, http://nytimes.com/2008/08/03/nyregion/nyregionspecial2/03principalsct.html (accessed November 21, 2010).

48. Gary Gordon, "Teachers Stick with Great Principals, Great Schools," *Gallup.com*, February 24, 2004, http://gallup.com/poll/10759/Teachers-Stick_Great-Principals-Great-Schools.aspx (accessed October 26, 2010).

49. Gary Gordon, "Teacher Retention Starts with Great Principals," Gallup.com, February 17, 2004, http://www.gallup.com/poll.10657/Teacher-Retention-Starts-Great-Principals.aspx/versi (accessed October 26, 2010).

50. University of Texas, "About 70 Percent of New High School Principals Leave within Five Years, Study Says," *University of Texas at Austin News*, October 5, 2009, http://www.utexas.edu/news/2009/10/05/prncipalretention/ (accessed November 15, 2010).

51. Herszenhorn, "Veteran Teachers."

Chapter 6

Workforce Strategies Needed to Mentor Failing Novice, Mid-Career, and Veteran Teachers

As I write this in April 2011, there is a great deal of turmoil in the education world. As *Bloomberg News* reports, "Public school teachers are facing the biggest threat to their job security in more than half a century as politicians target seniority rules that make the last hired fired when jobs are cut. . . . Officials are demanding the right to keep the most talented even if they have the least experience. . . . Superintendents contend that seniority rules force them to retain incompetent teachers instead of young talent." And Secretary of Education Arne Duncan said, "Layoffs based only on seniority don't help kids. We have to minimize the negative impact on students."[1]

But this kind of polarizing language only serves to divide older and younger teachers, administrators who value and need the experience of veteran teachers and those who are being pressured to buy out veteran teachers, and concerned parents and citizen groups. It's a polarizing effect that often leads to no improvement in teacher performance or exiting of incompetent teachers. It's a political sell that sounds good. It's a sell that elects and keeps politicians in office. Teachers have become the new target for politicians, and there is no relief in the campaign to discredit them. In the end it brings only more division and harm to the effort to improve teacher performance. Attacks don't help solve problems.

As *Bloomberg* reports, David Abbott, executive director of the George Gund Foundation, which supports education initiatives, appears to agree. Gund says that eliminating last-in, first-out rules isn't the solution, that what education needs is innovation. "There's too much emphasis placed on that issue as a silver bullet. We say, 'if we can just get rid of that work rule, of this industrial mentality, that will solve our problem.' No, it won't."[2]

Abbot speaks to the major argument of this book, that we need to be about improving the skills of all our teachers—novices, mid-career, and veterans. There are failing teachers in every segment of our school staffs. Some have very poor skills and need to be counseled out of the profession for their own good as well as the good of the students, parents, and colleagues. But many of these failing teachers can be retrained and supported through mentoring, modeling, and counseling by highly skilled veteran teachers. That's the innovation within our reach.

In order to bring this new staffing model into the schools, we need to replace the current school culture with a new narrative. The current culture says,

- The career span of teachers concludes at retirement age, no matter now skilled a teacher is.
- Early buyouts of all teachers approaching retirement only hasten their exit.
- The majority of teachers from every segment of the school staff—novice, mid-career, and veteran teachers, as well as administrators, parents, community members, even students—have bought this model. It's the way it's done.
- The exit of veteran teachers, even the highly skilled, will create many new jobs for younger teachers, without loss. This is a win-win situation. Veteran teachers get a buyout and novices get a job. The loss of the experienced will be overcome by eager and energetic new recruits.

That model represents an out-of-date culture doomed to failure in today's world. It's not innovation. It's a culture guaranteed to increase the number of failing and incompetent teachers. There's no one left in the school to turn to when trouble arrives in the classrooms of these new recruits, novices who are often facing assignments in the most challenging schools because that's where the openings exist, with little or no support.

Thomas G. Carroll and Elizabeth Foster say that schools are filling with inexperienced teachers, as the loss of veteran teachers is resulting in an experience gap for schools. They write,

In 1987–1988, the modal experience level was 15 years; the typical teacher had 15 years of experience and we had a robust pool of teachers with well over ten years of experience. By 2007–08 the mode was just 1–2 years of experience; 25% had five or fewer years of experience and 50% had 11 or fewer years of experience. [In] Massachusetts . . . the base of experienced teachers is approaching retirement, leaving the Commonwealth's high quality public education system in the hands of teachers with only a few years of experience and a propensity toward mobility into other professions.[3]

As a result, the pool of would-be mentors is rapidly diminishing. Now schools are facing a dire situation in which there is no intervention available when teachers of every segment of the school staff can't overcome these troubles and slide into cycles of failure. Teachers are on the road to being incompetent in spite of what the school district's public relations bulletins often say, that staff development experts are available to help teachers in crisis.

What teacher, no matter how bad their plight, want to call the district office and say, "I need help"? That's a fast way to raise a red flag and place you on the at-risk, endangered list. Instead we need to create a new narrative whose centerpiece is an updated staffing model with the following characteristics:

- We need the knowledge, skills, and experience of highly skilled veteran teachers to serve as mentors, coaches, and trainers; they must join with school administrators in helping teachers who continue to fail to find another, more rewarding, career.
- To do that we need to create new roles and benefits that will give them a reason to stay on board.
- These new roles will serve to reeducate our highly skilled staff from every segment that extending their career span is necessary to the school district, administrators, colleagues, students, and parents. They are our most valuable resource.
- These new roles will also serve to reeducate and sell school board members, administrators, teaching staff, parents, and citizens on the long-term value of retaining our highly skilled veteran teachers.

This model is an important innovation for the following reasons:

- It retains highly skilled veteran teachers as mentors.
- Other veteran teachers can choose retirement if they wish, thus creating positions for new hires.
- Ongoing training and retraining is now readily available for all staff, particularly young and inexperienced teachers who often face assignments in the most challenging schools because this is where the openings are.
- New mentors can become partners with overwhelmed administrators in helping incompetent teachers reassess their careers as teachers and consider a new career path. No one likes to fail. But they do need help and support to find a better path to success.
- It avoids the current political rhetoric of the last-hired, first-fired rules. Terms like "last hired, first fired," "incompetent teachers," and "seniority rules" are emotionally laden words that, as David Abbott suggests, will not contribute in a positive way to new innovations. They serve only to set up barriers.

In fact, these emotionally charged slogans that cause division mask the real issues blocking innovation: how to lift the performance of all teachers and how to aggressively intervene and counsel incompetent teachers into considering a career change. In my observations, we have failed to deliver on both counts. We are unable to increase the performance of all teachers because we lack the leadership role of mentors such as PS 35's Lori Gordon and Lauren Koster. And we lack the aggressive intervention and counseling process to confront incompetent teachers after all efforts to improve their skill have failed.

Skilled veteran teachers can deliver on both counts and not let the argument that seniority rules force education leaders to retain incompetent teachers instead of hiring young talent stand as gospel. Teachers can be trained to be effective and, for some, to become great teachers. But someone in the school hierarchy has to be given this role as backup to the building administrator.

And incompetent teachers can be counseled into assessing just how unsuccessful they are as teachers and be helped out of their cycle of failure with dignity, not blamed for the lack of skills but rather encouraged to accept the reality that this isn't the job for them. They should be given this option rather than being left alone, as Harry Walker was, to endure a professional life that offered him only pain and rejection. Someone in the school hierarchy has to be given this role as a backup to the building administrator.

In both the above cases, that someone is a highly skilled and experienced educator who can bring to the table skills as a leader, mentor, coach, , and counselor. Highly skilled veteran teachers with years of experience in the classroom can come to the aid of incompetent teachers when they assume a new role as mentor. They've seen many come and go in their careers, some who might have survived with the support that mentoring can offer. They know from firsthand experience that the word "incompetent" masks the real struggle that failing teachers experience.

Webster defines incompetent as "unskilled, without adequate ability, knowledge, fitness, failure to meet required standards, incapable." That's not the kind of skill repertoire teachers need when they enter the hurly-burly classroom world. If they are novice teachers they are at high risk from day one. At the other end of the spectrum, experienced teachers can also be at high risk if they were once successful but now find themselves in rapid decline.

In my observations any teachers—novice, mid-career or veteran—can one day find themselves unable to successfully respond to the daily demands from students, colleagues, administrators, parents, and their own expectations. They can find themselves in downward spirals, unable to meet required standards, and increasingly viewed by the school community as incapable. Years of experience, past successes, age, and college degrees don't matter much when the bottom falls out in one's personal and professional life.

Again, in my observations, it is the deadly combination of confronting hard times in one's home and school life that can render vulnerable teachers incompetent. Peoples' problems don't magically go away without intervention; they usually get worse. It's the same for teachers.

The following is a vignette that focuses on the role of the skilled veteran teacher as mentor. It's taken from the second edition of my book, *An Administrator's Guide to Better Teacher Mentoring*. This vignette focuses on the role of the teacher as mentor. Here we see some specific mentoring characteristics I identified in chapter 3 of that book:

- Mentors understand that a teacher's personal problems, such as divorce or a growing addiction, impact on the teacher's effectiveness and well-being.
- Mentors know how to listen, be nonjudgmental, and provide useful feedback and modeling.
- Mentors have knowledge about aging and barriers to career development.
- Mentors understand that renewing oneself is hard work; it's often not simple or even sought after.
- Mentors know how to take care of themselves and be physically and emotionally up to the mentoring task.
- Mentors value the loyalty and privacy of the protégé.
- Mentors know how to bring a sense of joy, energy, humor, and lightness to the mentoring relationship.

This vignette describes a relationship between mentor and teacher Frank Bronkowski and his protégé, math teacher Ellen Turner. Frank, a veteran twenty-year English teacher is in his first year as a mentor. He has been a very successful teacher and coach.

Coming to the school fresh out of college, he quickly established himself as a class act, an effective classroom teacher who is great with kids, a colleague others seek out for advice, and a teacher committed to working with kids after school as a basketball coach and faculty advisor.

He also continued his own learning experience, acquiring a master's degree plus. He now serves as adjunct professor in a local university's education department and recently coauthored a book on how teachers can help teens solve personal problems.

Frank was clearly an easy choice for the mentoring program. Still, the mentoring position is a new and challenging one for him. He has two periods each day for mentoring. While he has a gifted permanent sub, he continues to oversee her work, teach two classes himself, coach, and participate in weekly mentoring team meetings. He thanks God that he has a stable, caring home life that offers him support. And he is in excellent physical shape, running five miles a day.

Ellen has had a rockier career. She is in her thirtieth year of teaching, coming to the school fresh out of a master's program in 1972. For the first twenty-five years she was a school leader, teaching the more difficult math classes, administering the tutoring center after school, and working on a Ph.D.

But for the past five years she has seemed to withdraw from all activities except her classroom teaching; she has given up on her long-sought Ph.D. and turned the tutoring service over to younger teachers. Consequently, her teaching has suffered. Her department chair assigns only the most basic classes. She has started to miss school, calling in sick at least once every few weeks. The administration is considering requiring her to bring a doctor's note to verify her so-called illnesses. She doesn't look well and rumors say she is drinking heavily and is seen at a local liquor store each evening.

What happened to this once energetic, gifted teacher? The faculty room gossip says she's turned into a nightmare teacher, poorly prepared and unable to be an effective disciplinarian. Gossip also suggests that she has home problems. For the past three years she has been involved in a hostile divorce. Close friends say her marriage has been on the rocks for years. She increasingly isolates herself, arriving at school at the last possible moment, eating lunch in her room, and as one administrator puts it, "She is out of the parking lot before the buses leave."

The school's administration and some of her colleagues are very concerned for her well being but they seem unable to help her, somehow not able to find the right words. It is sometimes easier for teachers to help troubled kids than colleagues. There are other teachers who are not so kind. They mock her behavior in the faculty room and even have placed bets on how long she will be able to survive.

Some teachers are not so kind when they see a colleague in trouble. Does it create uneasiness in them, an uneasiness that suggests that this could happen to them someday? To them it is better to make a mockery of it, to make the failing teacher the victim, rather than internalize their own fears and vulnerability.

Does the mentoring program offer some hope for Ellen? Clearly, Frank has a big challenge trying to help Ellen get back on the right track and fight for her professional and perhaps her personal life. She seems to have given up.

But how should a mentor give someone life? How does a teacher break through the depression and wake up to the reality that she is failing and failing fast? We all know teachers like Ellen who are in flight; they are not strangers to us. Yet, like Frank, we ask ourselves, "How do I help?" Like Frank, we are not counselors or therapists. Teachers are not certified as helpers.

But that doesn't have to matter. Everyone has helping skills. We know how to listen, be nonjudgmental, and provide feedback that can help shake and shape our colleagues in need. We can be helpful in our own unique way if we are willing to take the risks to intervene and be a loyal friend. We understand that problematic personal relationships of colleagues impact the teacher's effectiveness and well-being. And we understand, because we have been there ourselves.

Maybe the words a mentor uses to connect with someone like Ellen are not terribly significant. Maybe what is important is the effort, a willingness to try and in trying to be willing to accept the rebuffs and refusals. In trying, we learn by doing and hopefully find the right words that will have meaning to someone like Ellen.

Mentors need to remember that there are few instant successes in connecting with teachers headed for trouble. The red light of danger may be on but they don't see it or they choose not to see it. It is the job of mentors like Frank Bronkowski to have them see the warning lights and advise and direct them to sources of help. Let's see how Frank proceeds.

Frank is a master teacher and he has been trained as a mentor. He knows the drill. But being well trained and knowing the drill doesn't always prepare him for mentoring real people with real problems. Frank's first task in helping Ellen is to understand what is wrong and right in her classroom. Once he has this data he can make an accurate assessment and plan for intervention. Ellen's is a classroom that was once alive with an energetic, caring teacher and students at ease, knowing they were in a safe place but yet challenged. There were no negative criticisms, no accusations, no screaming; it was a class students looked forward to each day.

But now, as Frank is to see, it is a classroom in despair, a teacher screaming and name-calling, a classroom inhabited only by students who have no way out, no parent to rescue them by complaining to the principal or counselor and demanding another teacher. It is a classroom in which the teacher—Ellen Turner, who almost has a Ph.D.—and her students have no way out. The only escape is for the teacher to call in sick and the students to cut class. Who will care if they do?

A VIEW OF ELLEN'S CLASS

Picture a classroom in despair: the bulletin board holds pictures yellowed with age describing events long past; a blank chalk board looks strangely unused for a ninth grade consumer math class; desks are spread out around the back of the room with no order, no rows, pushed as far away from the teacher's desk as possible. Ellen's desk seems isolated, not part of the classroom at all. The students slowly drift into class, many of them late, minutes after the final bell.

Although the class enrollment is twenty-two students, only fourteen are present. Ellen, sitting at her desk, seems to ignore what is going on, waiting for the kids to sit down. Five minutes into the class she takes attendance. When she calls out the names of absent students, the response of other students is often, "She cut."

Sometimes the students deliver quick, insulting remarks such as, "I don't know why I'm here. This class sucks." Or, "How come Fred got transferred to

Ms. Eglin's class? Probably his parents got him out. I wish my parents would do that. I agree with Sandra. This class sucks. We're not learning anything."

Ellen is unresponsive to the insults and challenges to her authority. She doesn't even seem to mind that her mentor, Frank, is observing this fiasco. It's almost as if she is saying, "Who cares what these kids do or what I do? I certainly don't any more. These kids are the bottom of the barrel. Teaching consumer math is the lowest of the low. I can't get much lower." She passes out a worksheet and says, "Do problems one through six in class and finish the rest for homework. If you fail to turn in the worksheet tomorrow it's an automatic failure."

One student named Mike interrupts: "What if you're not here? You're always out on Fridays. You sure get sick a lot. It's a wonder they still pay you."

Ellen, seeming oblivious, returns to her desk. The students quickly begin fooling around, throwing papers out the window. They look at Frank in a somewhat embarrassed way as if to say, "We know we shouldn't be doing this but Ms. Turner doesn't care so why should we?"

Minutes before the bell the students get up and leave. Ellen doesn't challenge them, telling them to stay in their seats until the bell. Frank thinks it's a miracle that the students hadn't acted out even more. Ellen established no control or boundaries, and demonstrated no preparation or interest.

Was Ellen really that oblivious to all the chaos in her classroom? Clearly she knows the difference between good and bad teaching. She was an effective teacher at one time. Frank wondered how she had arrived at this point. What happened to her pride? Her skills? Her craft? How did she develop such a tolerance for pain?

An unskilled mentor's view of this class rightfully sees disorder and chaos. But he misses the opportunity to help Ellen Turner become a more effective teacher. Ellen is lucky she doesn't have someone unskilled as her mentor; she might be out the door. An unskilled mentor might say, "Some way has to be found to get rid of Ms. Turner. Medical leave, whatever. Let's find a way and quickly. This lady is in trouble and we are not a clinic or rehab. We don't have the time or resources to coddle her. Let's call her in and encourage her to resign or apply for medical leave. I don't care that she was once a great teacher. The past doesn't matter. She's killing the kids. I know the union will go along with us."

Fortunately, Ellen has Frank Bronkowski as her mentor. Frank has a plan to help. He knows that there has to be a good reason for this decline in Ellen's performance. He feels that the best approach is to go to Ellen in the one-on-one conference with what he has observed as problems and get her to react. He'll do it gently, of course, but will accept no avoidance of issues.

He thinks, "Let's stop treating her as a patient. Let's forget about her divorce, isolation, even the drinking—if that rumor is true—and focus on classroom issues." He will leave Ellen plenty of room to bring up personal issues that may be draining her enthusiasm and energy, but the first step is to identify the classroom problem areas she needs to address.

Ellen is no dummy; she knows good teaching. He will remind her what that is and what it would take for her to get back there. Frank begins to wonder who is isolating whom. Has the school been isolating her, avoiding her? Was her seeming incompetence a cry for help? Frank sees opportunity here. He does not allow his students to become isolated and uncared for and Ellen will get the same treatment from him.

It is not hard for Frank to identify the problem areas that Ellen needs to work on. He lists his reflections on the problems and how he might address them in the conference:

1. Get some life into the classroom. Fix the bulletin boards. Bring in some flowers or pictures of your daughters and grandchildren.

2. Let your students know something personal about you, not your personal problems but something you're involved in. Do they know you started the tutoring program here? Many of your students get the help they need there. Think about going back to work there. It would be an ideal spot to help your students.

3. Find out something personal about your students. Sandra has just completed a great season with the soccer team. Mike has been doing some good stuff with the peer-counseling program. His dad passed away last summer and he is working with a group of elementary kids who have lost a parent. You have some interesting students. Many of them don't have much parental support but they're survivors, like you.

4. Let the students know you want them in class on time and they are not allowed to leave early. First, appeal to their good judgment. Say it looks bad for you and them if they are in the hall after the bell. If that doesn't work, give out detentions. Be tough. They'll respond.

5. Get rid of the worksheets and do some real teaching. You're putting the kids and yourself to sleep with the worksheets. You don't seem to care so why should they? You've been there. Use what you know.

6. Rearrange the desks so there is an emphasis on discussion. Give each student an assigned seat. No more back of the room isolation for them or you.

7. Create an atmosphere of self-respect and caring. Stop letting the students take pot shots at you. Stop the insults. Tell them you won't tolerate it any more. In turn you will respect them and treat them the same way. It will take a while because you've let it go on.

8. Get out of your room and start mingling with the staff. You've isolated yourself. I know some of our colleagues can be cruel and they criticize others to keep the heat off themselves. But keeping to yourself doesn't help you and it sparks unkind and malicious rumors. If you make yourself known people will talk less behind your back. Show your face.

9. What I am saying is to take back your classroom and your self-respect. We are going to work on this together. I know rebuilding pride isn't

easy. You're going to have to make some changes but that's OK. I'll be there as a loyal friend. What goes on between you and me stays here. I'll be loyal and respect your trust in me—if you'll give it to me. This will help me learn as a mentor. And who knows? Maybe this is a way for you to become a mentor someday. You're not the only struggling teacher in the building. You know that.

One-on-one conferencing following classroom observation is the heart and soul of the mentoring process. What kinds of conditions does Frank have to create? Consider the following suggestions:

If possible the meetings should be held in an attractive and comfortable environment, in an atmosphere of safety, trust, and professional respect. Protégés need to feel welcomed and affirmed and have a sense that this is a good place to be. Simple things can help humanize the mentoring setting: a pot of coffee, snacks, flowers on the table, comfortable seats. It should be a setting that encourages conversation. Ironically, these kinds of setting are rarely found in schools.

The environments in which we work often lack comfortable, professional spaces that allow for privacy, as educators often place all of their emphasis on the students and their needs. Professional comfort zones that can enhance conversation and professional dialog hardly exist. What we schools have is faculty rooms, often unkempt, with outdated, yard-sale furniture brought in by teachers.

Teachers settle for the minimum, as if they as educators aren't worthy of better conditions. This is a glaring example of teachers' inability to take care of themselves professionally, to demand more. Effective mentoring requires different, comfortable settings. Mentors need to create these kinds of comfort zones and learning hubs if they want their protégés to reflect on their teaching issues. Trying to carry on mentoring conversations in the anomie of the faculty room doesn't foster a feeling of privacy and safety.

In addition to creating an attractive setting, Frank needs to be ready to greet Ellen, raise critical issues, encourage her to respond, and develop an informal contract on how they will proceed as a team. Consider the following suggestions:

Bring some joy, energy, humor, and lightness to the meeting. Frank should greet Ellen with some positive feedback even if it's hard to find. His physical stance should be welcoming. He should smile, appear relaxed, and seem to be looking forward to the meeting.

Frank is good at asking questions that lead to reflection on Ellen's teaching process. He uses expressions like, "What is your take on what is happening? Here is what I see. Have you ever thought about . . . ? Here is how we might proceed. How does that sit with you?"

Frank gives homework assignments to both Ellen and himself. He might ask Ellen to write a reflection on how she views her teaching style, the positives and negatives, and how she views what work has to be done to improve. Frank suggests that he will do the same, take a look at his own teaching style. He also suggests to Ellen that she do a daily reflection on her teaching day, a reflection she can share with Frank if she chooses.

Using these hints Frank does not arrive at the meeting clueless. He has set the right conditions, he knows the right words to use to encourage communication, and he has a plan to help Ellen based on his classroom observations. This is how their conversation goes.

Frank: Hi, Ellen. Thanks for coming. Coffee? I got some great donuts at Hilda's bakery. Try one. Look, I am glad we could get together. As you know, this mentoring role is new for me. I want to be helpful if I can but I am not an expert by any means. I know every teacher has to be involved in the program but I want to keep this as simple and low-key as we can.

With that in mind, let me say that what we talk about and work on together stays between us. Brad Foley made it clear that this is not a supervisory situation. I am here to help . . . period. Maybe we could begin by my asking you how you view the program.

Ellen: Frankly, it's not something I want to be involved in. I've got other things to do. I also haven't been feeling too well lately so this is another burden. I am here because I have to be. I can't afford to jeopardize my job, especially right now. Frank, I like and respect you. You are a person I know I can trust, not like some other people in the building. But don't expect too much from me.

Frank: Sounds fair to me. I appreciate your honesty. Let me ask you how you think things are going in your classes. I've observed you three times and I've got some suggestions. But first I'd like to get your take on things.

Ellen: Whew, that's a tough one, particularly since I just told you that I'm not into this mentoring thing. Well, you're no fool, Frank. You see what's going on. I've just sort of caved in. I'm there. That's about it. Kind of weary of it all, I guess. And you're too nice a guy to bring it up but it's all over school that Rob and I have finally split up. Twenty-two years and the last few hell on wheels. I am just worn out. But money is tight and I can't afford to leave. Everyone's upset—me, my kids, my grandkids. I've got to sell my house and get an apartment. Jesus, I've lived there for twenty years. It's all I have and now that's gone too. But no one here seems to care. It's a mess and I'm a mess. You see it, the kids see it. I used to teach calculus and now they've stuck me with consumer math. I've become a nothing. Am I a burnout? I don't know. What a comedown.

Frank: I'm glad you're sharing this with me. Yes, it does look like you're struggling in the classroom and at home. It's a tough time. I'm glad I'm going to be around to support you. Part of mentoring is getting to talk about real life problems that may be affecting your teaching. And you are experiencing some tough ones. But, as you say, you also seem to be experiencing feelings that you've landed in a bad spot, dropped from calculus to consumer math, and your home problems may indeed be making you weary, burned out maybe. I'm not a counselor or a therapist but it's easy to figure out why you're struggling in the classroom. There's not much joy around right now.

Ellen: You've seen it. I'm just letting things go in my classroom and that's not really helping me. It's making things worse, really. You can't imagine how ashamed I am when I go home each day. It's so painful to see me as I am now. My poor performance only adds to my woes. I think if I enjoyed teaching and the kids once again, I would be a lot happier, but I can't seem to get started in that direction. I've got no one to talk to, except maybe you. I don't know. I'm open to any suggestions. This is killing me.

Frank: I think you're right. Working on some ways to improve your teaching may be the way to go. It may give you some uplifting success and increase your feeling of self-worth, which I sense has taken a beating. My sense is that it will probably take a while for your home issues to work out. Getting some counseling might help but I'm sure you've thought of that. It might take some of the burden off your shoulders. Having someone to talk to does help. But I think there are some things you can work on right now to begin to get back to your best teaching self. You've been there. You know what good teaching is.

I have some suggestions that might help you. Let me share them with you and see if you agree. Am I on target? Some of the suggestions are quite simple and I don't think you have to make a lot of major changes. Try brightening up your classroom with pictures and flowers. It'll help you and the kids. Let the kids know you have been having a tough time—you don't have to get into the details—and you're trying to change things. Think about rejoining the tutoring service or some other activity so you can get out and see people.

The peer-counseling program is looking for facilitators to help lead a divorce group. It may be just what you, and kids experiencing divorce, need. You're there; you know how hard it is. Get to know your students on a more personal level. Ask about their lives outside of school. Who knows? Some of them may be experiencing a divorce, too.

Also, set some rules and boundaries in the classroom. Expect the students to arrive and leave on time. Get a little angry and demand respect. You don't need to be talked down to. You may be weary but that doesn't mean you have to take crap, excuse my English. Rearrange the desks for discussion. Get back to questioning. Using worksheets, in my opinion, is not adding zest or creativity.

Think about how else you can reach these kids. You're a pro. You've been there. Get that bright and experienced mind of yours going. Think about getting out of your room for lunch. Stop letting people think you're troubled. Don't let them label you. The more you're out talking with others, the better it will be for you. Sure, you're having a rough time, but so are a lot of other teachers and administrators. Life hits us all.

Also think about writing a reflection on your teaching every day. It might help you focus on what's going on and how you're doing. And finally, think about counseling. It might help shore things up as you make changes. It might also help you find the words to talk about what's going on with your kids, grandkids and colleagues. Finally, I wrote these things out for you. If you want to take them with you, great. It's a list of things we might both work on. What do you think?

Ellen: You're right. A lot of these things are very simple but it does feel like too much to do all at once. Maybe I could just start with the room. I've got some great pictures of my kids and grandkids. Funny, I don't think I've ever shared anything about them with my class. I also have a great garden with lots of flowers. Gardening is a passion and hobby with me. It makes me feel at peace. I'll bring some flowers in, maybe even try to tell my students about my garden and what it means to me. Maybe I'll even make a lesson out of it, the profitability in professional gardening.

Look, Frank, this has been very helpful. I dreaded coming here. Even thought about calling in sick. But thank God I am here. Let me take the list and see what I can do before we meet again. I appreciate your concern for me and your offer to help. You really listened to me, got me to think, and your suggestions make sense. It's the first time in a long time that I've felt a little energy and hope that things can change. I just got through reading an article last night called "The Kindness of Friends." You certainly are one. Thanks.

Perfect ending? Who knows? Time will tell. But for this day, this moment, Ellen has some hope that things can improve. She has a little energy and a pulse. Without the well-thought-out and skilled intervention of Frank, chances are that things would have only gotten worse for Ellen. But now she has a trusted, loyal friend and some concrete issues to work on. She is not left to deal with her demons alone.

And Frank has the positive feedback he needs to reinforce his self-worth and mentoring skills. He sees that his effective questioning can result in reflections that make his protégé more aware of her teaching self, the good and the bad, and the work that needs to be done.

Where does someone like Ellen go if her school does not support mentoring? Some lucky ones find angels and saviors, or they save themselves. But most slip away, some silently—"She just called in and said she wasn't coming back. I knew she had problems but this is so sudden. Who do we have to fill her spot?"

Others, though, exit their school with a bang: "I knew it was going to happen. I could see it coming, that one day she was going to lose it. It was that seventh period class with all the difficult kids. She just exploded, started screaming and cursing and then she ran out of the building. Everyone—the kids, the teachers, the aides—was watching. Her ex-husband called last night and said she wasn't coming back. I wish we could have done something but we're no miracle workers."[4]

This is an example of the kind of professional intervention that skilled teachers such as Frank Bronkowski can deliver in their new role as mentor. Frank's role is a combination of mentor, therapist, confronter, supporter, and colleague/friend. His task is to raise Ellen Turner's self-awareness and help her to plan and implement new career goals that can help reverse her downward spiral. Frank is Ellen's partner, guiding her on the road to recovery. In a sense Frank's role and commitment is a therapeutic one, staying with Ellen as she decides whether or not she wants to change her life for the better and regain her winning stride with students and colleagues. He represents her lifeline to survival, somebody in the school who is charged, along with the principal, to be a doer, not an observer or critic of her failing situation.

Frank's intervention with Ellen Turner, as Lori Gordon's mentoring of Jewellyn Holder, puts a real face on why new mentoring roles are needed for skilled veteran teachers and why their intervention is desperately needed by beginning and experienced teachers who are trying to survive and get better at their craft.

However, as I mentioned earlier, taking on a new mentoring role, even part-time, can be threatening. The mentor has one foot in the classroom and the other in a semi-supervisory role. Neither fish nor fowl. Neither a full-time teacher nor a full-time supervisor. This is a new role not often seen in the school culture. So there have to be some benefits in addition to increased pay to encourage skilled teachers to take this risk. Altruistic reasons such as sharing one's skills with teachers in need in order to improve the school's overall performance may work well. I have also found that some successful teachers need to be challenged, conveying to them that they can no longer sit on the sidelines and watch teachers fail, given their skills to help, their being called to serve.

The streets are filled with fired ex-teachers who naively entered the profession hoping to encounter docile students, no bullies, peaceful classrooms without acting out or confrontational students, total acceptance and respect by students, and playgrounds absent of fights and name-calling. They were unprepared and paid the price. Hope simply is not enough to be a classroom teacher.

In the end survival comes before proficiency. In order for novice teachers to successfully navigate the path from survival to proficiency, they require the easily accessible, ongoing support of training offered by mentoring.

New part-time roles are beginning to be created for skilled veteran teachers who want to remain in the classroom and be involved with kids, rather than retire full-time. We are on the cusp of change with teachers who have a passion to remain actively involved as they age. Retiring teachers Gene Doxey and Jim Whitson provide such an example.

In Ramona, California, in 2004 these two teachers decided to return part-time as a teaching team out of their dedication to the students. "I'd really miss the kids," Doxey said. "I think the kids are the most important reason I'm here. I enjoy the interaction and working with this age group." Doxey had been with the Ramona Unified School District for twenty-six years.

Whitson, for thirty-one years, taught world history to seventh-graders. The contemporary issues class he took on was a new experience for him but one he welcomed.[5]

Here are two gifted teachers who found a way to continue their work with children while at the same time the San Diego Unified School District was negotiating incentives for the most experienced teachers to retire early, enticing seasoned teachers to leave the payroll and replacing them with lower-paid novices.

What we need to be after is changing the culture of the school so that it normalizes a process to retain skilled veteran educators. We need to create a career path that makes excellent sense given that people want to work longer and organizations need their experience, skills, knowledge, and wisdom.

Sheila and Letty Sustrin's fiction book, *The Teacher Who Would Not Retire*, describes in a humorous yet passionate way how such a career path evolved for Mrs. Belle, a first-grade teacher. The Sustrins, both retired teachers, know firsthand about the pressure on older teachers to retire and make way for newcomers. The story they tell shows how older teachers can resist these efforts and remain where they belong—in their classrooms.

The story focuses on Mrs. Belle, s first-grade teacher at Laurelville Town School. The children loved her. She always smiled and spoke softly to them. She had ten pairs of ballet slippers in her closet and each day she wore a different color and danced around the room as the children sang, "We see you here! We see you there! We see your slippers everywhere!"

But all this happiness came to an end the day Mr. Rivera, the principal, came to Mrs. Belle's classroom. He said, "Mrs. Belle, you know how we all love you. I am sorry, but I have to tell you that you must retire."

Mrs. Belle shouted, "What? Retire? Why? Who will teach the children that learning the alphabet and numbers can be fun? I must be there to read them their favorite stories. I cannot stop coming to school."

Mr. Rivera said, "The School Rules say you are too old to teach at this school. Now you can stay home and rest. Please pack your things because the new teacher comes tomorrow."

As the story evolves, Mrs. Belle finds creative ways to stay in contact with "her" children. At first she becomes a window washer outside the classroom; the children recognize her immediately because she is wearing pink ballet slippers. The children sing, "We see you here! We see you there! Hooray! Mrs. Belle is back."

Mr. Rivera tells Mrs. Belle she must leave and has a security guard walk her away from the school. The next day she appears as a new food server in the cafeteria. She doesn't look like Mrs. Belle, but she is wearing green ballet slippers. Again the children sing, and again Mr. Rivera tells her she must leave. She goes on to play the role of a helper to the fire inspector at the school for a fire drill, and is shown the door once again.

The tide turns in Mrs. Belle's favor when Mr. Rivera finds himself engulfed by sacks of mail from parents saying they don't want her to retire. Mr. Rivera has no choice but to create a new role for Mrs. Belle. At a meeting with the parents he says, "Our school board has a very special job for Mrs. Belle. From now on every Friday will be 'Mrs. Belle Day' at Laurelville Town School. We have made a cozy corner in our library and we will invite Mrs. Belle to read her favorite stories to the children."

The story has a happy ending: "Every Friday you can find Mrs. Belle reading books to the children in Mrs. Belle's Reading Corner. And, of course, she always wears her ballet slippers."[6]

Mrs. Belle's belief in her value to "her" children and parents and determination to find creative ways to remain in their lives despite rigid work rules is the kind of model we need to emulate. While the Sustrins' story is fiction, they know as teachers for thirty-eight years, teaching side by side in the same school district, the pressures that can be put on the Mrs. Belles of the teaching world to retire. But as this story shows, teachers who believe in their own skills and the value they bring to students can demand a second opinion and flexible work alternatives. Like Mrs. Belle they have earned our respect and deserve a place at the table if they choose to remain on board and contributing, not shown the door, told to pack up or "stay home and rest."

But the Mr. Riveras of the education world deserve our understanding as well. In the highly pressurized world of today's schools, building principals can also be victims of antiquated work rules that arbitrarily determine retirement policies with no regard to retaining highly skilled teachers such as Mrs. Belle. Often building principals have to act against their own self-interest and encourage skilled teachers, the cornerstone of the school staff, to retire because there are no flexible, part-time roles in the organization. As Thomas G. Carroll and Elizabeth Foster have pointed out, teachers are often forced to make career decisions based on their retirement plan's benefits and penalties to the detriment of teaching quality in their schools.

Some teachers stay in teaching when they probably should go, just to get the next "bump up" in pension benefits that add wealth to their pension fund. Others, who are accomplished veterans, retire when they would rather stay in order to maintain the best employment benefits. Carroll and Foster suggest that antiquated retirement policies cannot adapt to relevant shifts in school staff needs and in fact often act in contradiction to efforts to develop and maintain a high-quality teaching workforce.

Creating new roles for older teachers can also remove a great burden for building principals and press school districts to rethink the pension benefits that often lead teachers who should go to stay, and accomplished veterans who would rather stay to leave for the best retirement benefit. Carroll and Foster argue that

eliminating barriers to returning to work after retirement would enable principals and districts to retain or rehire experienced master or other highly qualified teachers to build a balanced team of veteran and newer teachers, creating new roles for accomplished veteran teachers who could coach and mentor novice teachers. . . .

The National Board for Professional Teaching Standards has a well-tested process for defining and recognizing effective teachers and then helping them collaborate and take on leadership roles. Adapting this type of framework to include input from schools about their specific needs and using mutually agreed-upon processes to offer teachers approaching retirement new opportunities would result in a cadre of effective experienced teachers eager to support 21st-century teaching and learning.[7]

Carroll and Foster recommend we need an alignment of retirement policies with workforce and educational goals. The "education leaders who are responsible for teaching quality and the policymakers responsible for retirement are not working with each other. As a result, teachers are too often whipsawed between conflicting goals and penalties of two different systems." They say "we need to create a new stage of life and work for experience professionals."[8] I submit we must institute a process that would focus the culture of the school of retaining, not abandoning, our older teachers, a process that would free the Belles and Riveras to be partners, not antagonists.

But these recommended changes are not going to happen overnight. Failing teachers and their students need our intervention now. There are important action steps we can take by expanding new roles, such as the PS 35 mentors, a role that involved two veteran teachers, employed part-time as mentors and classroom teachers, in one school setting. In this model mentoring is available on a daily basis for teachers in need. Help is a step away. They don't have to wait for help to arrive from district staff developers and building principals who are often overwhelmed. Nor do they have to wait for help from retired teachers who appear a few days a month to volunteer as mentors. A lot can happen to fledgling teachers in a month's time and it is often bad news.

Following is an example of an effort by well-intentioned people and organizations to help novice teachers. It does not deliver the degree of help novice and failing teachers need because it offers too little help over too long a time. Serving three or four hours a month as a mentor in a hectic high school setting is a patchwork intervention. Like many other mentoring programs, it sound good—volunteer mentors helping newly arrived novice teachers—but it lacks a coherent, day-by-day strategy.

Bernard Kobin returned recently to his old stomping grounds, Pasadena Muir High School, where he spent nearly two decades teaching driver ed, general typing, health and whatever else came his way. It wasn't a reunion that drew the 81-year-old Glendale resident and his wife Sadie, also a former high school teacher. They were there to serve as mentors to first-year teachers Judy Hu and

David Herman, both members of Teach for America. . . . "I'm going to draw
on my experience," said Bernard. . . . "If it works I'll be happy. If not, we'll try
something different."[9]

Bernard mentored David Herman, a math and science teacher. Sadie mentored Judy Hu, an English teacher, which was set up by UCLA's Center on Aging, which has retired teachers and administrators volunteer in the Teach for America program.

While the Kobins are dedicated people and novices such as Hu and Herman seem to benefit from their help, this model simply can't pass muster as a creditable mentoring effort. Why? Because it sets forth a model that doesn't deliver the easily accessible help that novice teachers need. It's a model that offers a good news story but in reality offers only a small dose of help. Is this an effective approach to help newcomers? I say no. Let's avoid developing mentoring programs that, although they sound good, are simply patchwork efforts that avoid solving the often daily problems faced b novice and failing teachers.

We need to begin the change process emphasizing a creditable model for new roles for veteran teachers. We need a low-cost approach that gives veteran teachers such as PS 35's Lori Gordon and Lauren Koster reasons to stay and benefits that sweeten their decision to stay. We need to nurse, support, and shine the light on these new roles for veteran teachers as a strategy to educate educators that the current school culture is limiting our options to improve the performance of all our teachers as well as our organizations' problem-solving mechanism.

Many highly successful teachers are after rewards in addition to financial compensation. Successful teachers want new challenges and risks that let their creative energies flow and open doors to new learning. However, when challenges, risks, and opportunities for new learning fail to exist for veteran teachers and monetary rewards become the only reason to stay or go, we have in effect signed off on older teachers as vital staff members. We've orchestrated a slow professional and, sometimes, personal death for them.

In the culture of the school, as in many organizations, solutions that worked in the past are seen as the only option. One teacher who was resisting reform efforts told me, "It's the way things are done here. Don't come into our school and make waves. We may not be perfect but we certainly don't need a house call from doctors like you." Things don't change unless a crisis erupts, and even then there are no guarantees. People, educators included, tend to stay with what they know in both their personal and private lives, for good or for bad. Breaking up is hard to do, even when the personal or professional relationship is failing.

Sarah Edith Fiarman et al. supply some reasons as to why the culture of the school has succeeded in resisting any major efforts to alter teacher staffing.[10] They say the teaching career has historically been "flat," with unwavering job responsibilities. Unlike other professions, teachers typically do not take on new responsibilities outside their classrooms as they gain experience and skills. A norm of "egalitarianism" continues to exist where all appear equally skilled, thus the idea that a teacher may have greater expertise is resisted by peers, who question their role. Peers ask, "What makes you better than the rest of us?" and "What gives you the right to tell me what to do?"

Fiarman et al. cite a 1986 report by the Carnegie Forum of Teaching and the Economy, "A Nation Prepared," recommending new positions for lead teachers to provide career development for teachers.

One reason this effort faded over time is that lead teachers often experienced uncomfortable relationships with peers in their new roles. Instructional leadership roles have increased in number, but such roles continue to be difficult to carry out, particularly where critical feedback to improve their peers' instruction is involved. To appear less threatening, lead teacher thus often soften their feedback, which limits their effectiveness.

The school culture as we know it has established a pattern of interactions that influences how the individuals in it behave. The set of behaviors it fosters under what Fiarman et al. label as "egalitarianism" has had a chilling effect on teachers and innovation. She describes a culture in which teachers are afraid to take on new roles even though they are highly skilled and qualified.

On the battleground of school reform it has an appearance similar to that of the bullying experienced by students. Bullying peers tend to put a student "in their place" if he or she appears to be "different." It's the same for some teachers, who employ bullying tactics to stifle change. When a peer starts to be "different," seeking out a new role to demonstrate his or her expertise, resisting teachers strike back. Fiarman uses words such as "frustrated," "rebuffed," "uncomfortable," and "threatened" to describe how teacher leaders feel in dealing with peers. I would add the words "frightened," "misunderstood," "betrayed," "victimized," "failing," and "angry" to her list.

There is this dark side to educational reform that is rarely talked about. In my experience teachers taking on new roles often find themselves the targets of bullying tactics by other teachers. They usually don't anticipate the assaults on their professional and personal lives that will come. They have entered, albeit with good intentions, a hostile environment where they are called names, made fun of, ridiculed, made victims of nasty personal and professional rumors, isolated, and shunned from social activities.

I know it well. It's not a role for the faint of heart. Teachers who use bullying tactics to fight change often win the battle. They literally frighten ambitious peers away from being successful in new roles. They've had a great deal of experience in saying "no" and causing mischief and disharmony. The lessons are not lost on other highly skilled teachers who may have similar ambitions for leadership and mentoring roles. In this culture everyone loses except the aggressor—the would-be leader and mentor, the failing teachers who need their intervention, students who have to suffer through classes in turmoil, administrators who need the involvement and support of teacher leaders, and parents who want the best teachers for their kids.

The current culture fosters hostile behaviors not only against potential teacher leaders and mentors but also against the belief that teachers should create close relationships and care about their students' wellness and personal lives as well as their academic development. The forte of highly resisting teachers is confrontation and fear, not support and development of a caring school community that can respond when a member becomes at risk and is heading toward the margins of school and community life.

If veteran teachers are going to be successful in new roles of mentoring, they need to have courage, the will to succeed and win, skills in confronting and overcoming resistance, political skills, the ability to promote and sell their cause, and a strong support system, all in addition to their mentoring skills. Political skills can help them to identify teachers who are supporting them, those on the fence, and those who are strongly opposed and will probably cause trouble. Their sales and promotional skills can help them sell colleagues, even the most resistant ones, on the value of their mission.

In my experience the major key to overcoming resistance has been to go directly to the turf of balking teachers, engage them in dialogue that tries to win them over and to repeat this polite confrontation until it hopefully reaches the point where a degree of mutual respect is established. Do not avoid the resisters or, as Fiarman et al. reported, soften the critical feedback.

The PS 35 model, in which two mentors work together and have the strong support of their principal, makes good sense. Three targets are harder to gun down than one solitary, overexposed mentor. With two mentors, one can play the good cop, working to maintain dialogue and open communication with resisting groups, while the other plays the role of bad cop, pushing ahead with the mission no matter how many arrows are hitting them.

There is a difference between honest resistance to change, in which every faculty member is given a voice in civil discussions, and resistance that is dominated by balking teachers, often self-centered individuals who don't want anyone else getting ahead, who will use any weapon, no matter how negative, to derail the process and the people involved. We see the latter too often in school reform efforts but that doesn't mean we should cease efforts to win them over and get them on board as participants.

It's easy to work with teachers who support you. Entering the lion's den to promote new roles may not be a walk in the park but it's something that has to be done. This intervention process is often successful because balking teachers don't expect school reformers to enter their turf. It's one way to gain their respect and establish a dialogue that avoids the game that is usually played—confrontation, name-calling, and mutual disrespect.

Sometimes simply showing up, sharing a cup of coffee or a beer, is the best way for education reformers to make their pitch. As in dealing with school bullies, you don't leave them alone to continue with their aggressiveness. You intervene and try to teach them alternative approaches to connecting with peers.

It's the same with resisting teachers. As education reformers we often learn valuable lessons from those who don't buy our change efforts. They make us work harder, sweat the resistance, and we go home on many nights feeling like failures. They wear us down until we want to give up, crawl away, or dilute our message so it becomes only a watered-down version of our original plan.

However, things can change for the better if the bullies' hostile blows are not returned with acrimony and teacher leaders courageously stay on their feet looking for openings for their message. As in sports, when time runs out and the game is tied, the two teams shake hands. The healing can begin now that the last shot has been taken and it falls short. Teachers, even the most arrogant, can tire of battling and will lay down their weapons if they see something they can relate to in the person who wants to change their world.

This culture has to change and will when we create new roles for veteran teachers, arm them with the necessary training to isolate unfounded personal and professional attacks, and provide them with strong protection, a safety net, in building and district administrators. In doing so we will have injected a winning formula to reframe the culture as a place novice and failing teachers can get the help they need to succeed and where skilled veteran mentors can shine the light on their individual worth and expertise. We can move the culture out of the dark where resisting teachers dominate the change agenda and concerned teachers feel intimidated and powerless, prisoners of a culture gone bad.

The new culture I am advocating will make it more attractive for veteran teachers to delay full-time retirement and sign on as leaders, mentors, coaches, and trainers. The need is there. In discussing emerging career opportunities in K-12 education, Elizabeth Foster suggests that teachers would stay if given new challenges or part-time opportunities.[11]

Foster's report examined different career pathways and found that 58 percent of teachers and 49 percent of administrators say that in their schools some teachers combine part-time teaching with other roles and 37 percent say they are interested in such a roles. The survey concludes that shifting demographics and the national emphasis on increasing student achievement and teacher quality are influencing careers in education as the retirement of Baby Boom teachers and other factors produce pressure and create opportunity. The survey also reports that three-quarters of teachers would like to continue to work in education beyond traditional retirement. There are hybrid positions emerging, and some highly skilled Baby Boomers are waiting to be invited to lead mentoring programs to reduce the attrition of new teachers arriving from nontraditional and traditional programs as well as helping failing teachers stop their path to becoming incompetent teachers.

The following is a voice from the school community who tells the story of what it's like to be waiting for such an invitation, one that would offer an incentive to stay in the district and a reward for being a high-quality professional. In my experience such invitations are in short supply. This voice laments the absence of rewards and recognition for older teachers.

In his letter to the editor of *Newsday* on January 31, 2011, William Lemmey, a retired teacher from the Hicksville Public Schools, wrote,

> This is in reply to Philip Cicero's opinion about laying off teachers with little regard for seniority. This would be a mistake. Senior teachers are usually the leaders of the school. They know how to manage a classroom, develop new curriculum, control the halls and supervise cafeterias. They often contribute to extra-curricular activities. If the district offers no seniority reward for career teachers, then what incentive does a high quality professional have to stay in the district? Districts would lose the sense of community that develops when senior teachers feel they have a bond with the students, parents, administrators, custodians, secretaries and other people in education.[12]

Veteran teachers like Lemmey need reasons and incentives to stay. They have an established bond with various segments of the school community. They know the nuts and bolts of a successful teacher's daily life, such as class management, curriculum development that engages students, control of and interaction with students in the hallways and cafeterias, and the importance of being involved with students in extracurricular activities. These are all separate but intertwined areas of a successful teacher's daily life that can easily become a series of nightmares for inexperienced and unskilled novice teachers absent ongoing mentoring and modeling that Lemmey might have offered instead of retiring.

Learning to teach is like learning to dance. Take one step here, the other there, over and over until you develop a rhythm and flow that guides you through the various challenges and changing roles involved in the teaching day—classroom teacher, hallway monitor, lunchroom supervisor, softball

coach. Each role requires a different set of skills along with a slightly different face and demeanor, skills learned one step at a time as a novice and often
accompanied by many failures and setbacks. If you're lucky you have a mentor,
a dance instructor, who says to you, "If you keep dancing and resist the urge to
give up, you'll eventually learn how to flow from one step to the next."

Susan Moore-Johnson and her colleagues say that new roles for teachers

> have long existed in American schools but were in short supply in the past. The
> department head position at the high school level is perhaps the most widespread
> and enduring . . . role. Recently new roles, such as mentor teachers, instructional
> coach, literacy coach and grade-level team leaders have emerged. . . . These
> roles may influence teachers in at least two ways. First, those who are less expe-
> rienced may perceive the role as a promising, future opportunity and thus decide
> to remain in schools and in the profession. Second, teachers who hold the roles
> may experience heightened job satisfaction and increased retention.[13]

Johnson says teacher satisfaction and retention are in large part due to the
support, or lack of it, teacher leaders receive while in the role. PS 35 teachers
Lori Gordon and Lauren Koster enjoy such critical support from Principal
Graciela Navarro.

Johnson et al. also cite research that "holding leadership roles may increase
teacher commitment to their schools and, if the roles are well-matched to the
individual's and offer skill variety, help them to avoid burnout. However, as
Johnson points out, "if schools fail to offer teachers support and opportunities throughout their careers, they risk losing them prematurely. . . . Research
indicates that experienced teachers desire programs—professional development, new roles and career ladders—that target their needs. . . . If schools
fail to respond to [these needs], . . . the loss may be particularly great among
those teachers who seek the expanded influence and responsibility most at
odds with the traditional course of the teacher career path and the traditional
organization of the schools.[14]

The good news is that there are new educational workforce models emerging that are challenging the traditional course of the teaching career path and
the traditional organization of the school, such as New York City's Teacher
Leader role.

Thomas G. Carroll and Elizabeth Foster suggest "learning teams" as
another closely connected model. They say,

> The traditional teaching career is collapsing at both ends. Beginners are being
> driven away by antiquated preparation practices, outdated school staffing poli-
> cies, and inadequate career rewards. At the end of their careers accomplished
> veteran teachers who still have much to contribute are being separated from

their schools by obsolete retirement systems. . . . Unless we act now, we will lose an unacceptably large number of our best educators, just as the largest generation of children in our history must gear up to assume its place in a complex world. We have less than a decade to develop a new education workforce strategy. The idea of a single highly qualified teacher in every classroom is an idea whose time has passed.

They suggest that one solution is developing collaborative learning teams composed of veterans and beginners sharing their expertise and experience with each other.

These learning teams will comprise many different roles, including teachers, coaches, and learning team leaders, online educators, mentors, and so on. Carroll and Foster say "these teams will provide the opportunity for veteran teachers phasing out of full-time teaching to give back to the school and students in a different kind of 'retirement,' while helping beginners to accelerate their progress toward effective teaching."[15]

The traditional school culture, with its blinders on, needs changing. It's preventing our schools from utilizing the resources at hand to tackle the problem of retention for novice teachers and professional growth for mid-career and veteran teachers. Schools are at risk for ongoing turmoil if leaders of policy and practice fail to intervene. But we do have new education workforce models at hand that can provide positive alternatives to the three-for-one epidemic.

This epidemic is a flawed process that poses a real danger for our students, parents, teachers and administrators. It's a high-risk scenario that is creating a school environment in which novices are leading the school agenda, blinded by inexperience. This is fertile territory for chaos and problem making, much like a dysfunctional family in which the parents have relinquished their parenting role to the kids. In this scenario no one is in charge or knows how to take charge, no one knows how to get help and solve problems, family members do their own thing, marching to their own drummers, and members are at high risk of failure and heading toward the margins of school and community life.

Wisdom has taken a path away from such schools and families and members will pay the price. Unfortunately the greatest burden will fall on students, who are innocent bystanders and who trust adults to make their world safe, peaceful, nourishing, and filled with opportunities. But as we have seen in this book, the trusted adults often get involved in their own world of survival, leaving little time or energy for reflection on why they came into teaching—to help kids and to prepare them to lead a life with good values, a strong work ethic and responsibility to their fellow man and woman.

It's not all the fault of these educators. They got detoured in their mission by the negative politics they found in school life, tough economic times and a nationwide antiteacher environment. We have the tools and skills to change that environment. We don't have to end up cheating kids out of a good education and teachers out of becoming great teachers. We know the answers. As Carroll and Foster urge, we have to act *now.*

Let me close by putting a real face on the kind of world gifted teachers inhabit—their love and caring for children, even the most difficult ones; the special place that children have in their professional and personal lives; and the love, affection, and life lessons that are returned to them from appreciative children. These teachers are able to quickly form deep personal relationships with each student at the beginning of the school year, relationships that serve as a foundation for the hard work involved in the learning now required.

Kate Bracken, a second-grade teacher, offers some wise advice on what is required to be a gifted teacher. Her story makes clear the important message that successful teachers love their job and their students. Their home away from home is their classroom and they feel blessed to be there, in the right place for them. To rob them of their careers through retirements would be an extremely destructive act against them and their students.

Allow me to share Ms. Bracken's story, which originally appeared in *Gig: Americans Talk about Their Jobs* by John Bowe et al.

> I was one of those people who was pretty much . . . unable to decide what they wanted to do with themselves. I didn't have any kind of long-term planning or anything. . . . I saw this teaching position advertised, an assistant for second grade. I lived right near the school . . . so I interviewed and they hired me. And that's how I got into teaching. But I was so thrilled by it. I mean, there were problems. . . . But I just loved the teaching thing—with even the worst kids there was something interesting and kind of lovely. I was really into it in a way that I just hadn't been into anything before.

But while terrified at first, Bracken goes on to say, "In a certain way I just feel blessed to have these kids, you know, in my life. They teach me, you know, they make me less nervous or something, I guess. . . . Basically, I just feel more comfortable with the world since I started teaching—and that comfort, you know, comes from hanging around kids. . . . I don't have any long-term plans except this. . . . I realized that I've been, like, redeemed by teaching. Like teaching is right for me. I'm a person who should be a teacher."[16]

Teachers like Kate love what they do and their children. They are in the classroom to stay, and as Kate tells us, she doesn't have any long-term plans. Teaching is right for her. She's not just putting in time until retirement or keeping her emotional distance from her children as some teachers do. Hers is an education workforce model that is quiet, personal, involved, supportive and accepting. Kate may be tired, may find some children difficult, and she had years that were less good than others, but she is confident now that she can succeed in her classroom.

Kate's teaching career offers another workplace model that's not from a research project or teacher preparation textbook. It's Kate's own version based on who she is and where she wants to be, to settle. It's a very humane model in which the teacher is not in a role but is herself, doing what she does best, in her way, and loving the way she delivers her unique style. The lesson here for future teacher leaders, mentor, coaches, trainers, and learning team members may be to capitalize on the special gifts that each teacher has and what makes each feel, like Kate, that teaching is right for them, even when they are terrified.

What is the "it" that makes their message, style and performance so powerful and irresistible? For our fictional Mrs. Belle, it was her ballet slippers, smile, and joy in being with her children. In the end there's no mystery here. Being a great teacher begins and ends with liking/loving kids, even the most difficult ones. If teacher leaders, coaches, trainers, and team members can train teachers that it's okay to be terrified of difficult students but—and it's a big but—also give them the skills to find something they can relate to, then they will be successful at their job. Their job is to develop the willingness and skills to teach these students instead of avoiding them because they are a threat to the teacher's comfort zone.

In my experience some mid-career teachers who balk at reform are also the ones who are terrified by difficult students. While they don't admit to being terrified, their reaction to uncooperative and different students is "out of here, go to the principal's office." In some situations dealing aggressively with acting-out students is the right call. But for many other students it's a macho response that says, "I'm in charge. These kids don't want to cooperate. I don't get paid to try to teach these kids who are uninterested in what I'm teaching. I want them out of there now."

These teachers who resist closer personal involvement with difficult students play a powerful role in the current school culture. Teacher leaders need to make them their first intervention priority. As in sports, you don't win games when the manager decides who plays and who doesn't based on which players he is most comfortable with. In the school game, coaches like Kate Bracken and Mrs. Belle succeed because they involve all their students as players and contenders.

This formula to involve hesitant and terrified teachers in closer personal relationships with difficult students is the same strategy teacher leaders need to use with difficult teachers who resist their message and balk at new roles for colleagues. Their job, again, is to find something the resisters can relate to in either their personal or professional lives and get them involved, give them the willingness and skills to overcome their resistance to change, not avoid them because they are a threat to the teacher leader's comfort zone.

If highly skilled and politically savvy veteran teachers can successfully accomplish this dual intervention role, the prospects for increasing student performance, teacher retention and positive career development for *all* teachers stand a good chance for success. This should be our goal but a goal tempered by the reality that teacher leaders will experience some failures in this dual process. The reward for teacher leaders, mentors, coaches, and trainers is in making their best effort to improve teachers' performance amid setbacks. It's critically important in today's school world because, as Carroll and Foster suggest, the idea of having a highly qualified teacher in every classroom is an idea whose time has passed.

We need to do our best to raise the performance bar of all teachers and not let it fall to dangerous levels. There is a tipping point that can lead to a negative school climate and if continued, to chaos. Not every teacher is going to be Mrs. Belle or Kate Bracken, but with mentoring and support they can be good enough to help kids or at least good enough not to hurt them. Using a sports analogy, not every player can hit 500 for the season, score thirty points in a game, or pitch a shutout game in every appearance. Some players have average skills, but with good coaching, self-motivation, and persistence, they find their way into the lineup and become starters. The job of teacher leaders is to emulate this coaching model.

NOTES

1. Oliver Staley, "Teacher Seniority Rules, Job Security, Threatened amid Budget Cuts," *Boston.com*, March 27, 2011, http://www.boston.com/nation/articles/2011/03/27/teacher_seniority_rules_job_security_threatened_amid_budget_cuts (accessed March 27, 2011).

2. Staley, "Teacher Seniority Rules."

3. Thomas G. Carroll and Elizabeth Foster, *Who Will Teach? Experience Matters* (Washington, DC: National Commission on Teaching and America's Future, 2010), 10.

4. William L. Fibkins, *An Administrator's Guide to Better Teacher Mentoring*, 2nd ed. (Lanham, MD: Rowman & Littlefield Education, 2011), 109–18.

5. Ruth Lepper, "Seven Teachers' Retirement End of an Era," *Sign On San Diego*, May 6, 2004, http://signonsandiego.printthis.clickability.com/pt/cot?action=cpt%title =Seven+teachers%2 (accessed September 1, 2010).

6. Sheila Sustrin and Letty Sustrin, *The Teacher Who Would Not Retire* (West Bay Shore, NY: Blue Marlin Publications, 2002).

7. Carroll and Foster, *Who Will Teach?* 18–20.

8. Carroll and Foster, *Who Will Teach?* 19–20

9. Sherry Joe Crosby, "Support System: Retired Teachers Team Up with New Ones," *The Free Library*, 1999, http://www.thefreelibrary.com/SUPPORT+SYST EM%3b+RETIRED+TEACHERS+TEAM+UP+WITH+NEW+ONES.-a083625050 (accessed October 15, 2010).

10. Sara Edith Fiarman et al, *Teachers Leading Teachers: The Experience of Peer Assistance and Review Consulting Teachers* (Cambridge, MA: Harvard Graduate School of Education, 2009), 1–3.

11. Elizabeth Foster, "How Boomers Can Contribute to Student Success: Emerging Encore Career Opportunities in K-12 Education," *Civic Ventures*, 2010, 5–7.

12. William Lemmey, "Senior teachers are the heart of the school," Letter to the Editor, *Newsday*, January 31, 2011, A22.

13. Susan Moore Johnson, Jill Harrison Berg, and Morgaen L. Donaldson, *Who Stays in Teaching and Why: A Review of the Literature on Teacher Retention* (Cambridge, MA: Harvard Graduate School of Education, 2005), 93.

14. Johnson, Berg, and Donaldson, *Who Stays in Teaching*, 97.

15. Thomas G. Carroll and Elizabeth Foster, *Learning Teams: Creating What's Next* (Washington, DC: National Commission on Teaching and America's Future, 2009), 2, 6

16. John Bowe, Marisa Bowe, and Sabin Streeter, *Gig: Americans Talk about Their Jobs* (New York, NY: Crown Publishers, 2000), 391–94.

Bibliography

Adler, Richard. "Special Report: Reinventing Retirement." *Civic Ventures*, December 2004. http://www.civicventures.org/publications/articles/reinventing_retirement.cfm (accessed October 18, 2010).

Alboher, Marci. "Discovering Second Acts in Sustained Working Lives." *New York Times*, February 11, 2008. http://www.nytimes.com/2008/02/11/jobs/1shift .html?ref=teach_for_America&pagewant (accessed October 16, 2010).

Allen, Scott. "North White Schools Buy Out 9 Teachers to Ease Budget Woes." *Herald Journal*, March 9, 2010. http://www.indianaeconomicdigest.net/main.asp/ (SectionalD=31&subsectionID=244&arti (accessed October 15, 2010).

Anderson, Nick. "Midwest Union Battles Highlight Debate over Improving Schools." *Washington Post*, March 3, 2011. http://washingtonpost.com/wp-dyn/content/ article/2011/03/2AR201103020314_pf (accessed March 11, 2011).

Auriemma, Frank V., Bruce S. Cooper, and Stuart C. Smith. *Graying Teachers: A Report on State Pension Systems and School District Early Retirement*. Eugene, OR: ERIC Clearinghouse on Education Management, 1992.

Bowe, John, Marisa Bowe, and Sabin Streeter. *Gig: Americans Talk about Their Jobs*. New York, NY: Crown, 2000. 391–94.

Brooks, David. "Tools for Thinking." *New York Times*, March 29, 2011. http://www .nytimes.com/2011/1/03/29/opinion/29brooks.html?_=1&hp=+pagewanted=print (accessed March 29, 2011).

Bryant, Adam. "The Quest to Build a Better Boss." *New York Times*, March 13, 2011.

Butler, Robert. *Ageism in America*. Report of the Anti-Ageism Task Force. New York, NY: International Longevity Center, 2006.

Carroll, Thomas G., and Elizabeth Foster. *Who Will Teach? Experience Matters*. Washington, DC: National Commission on Teaching and America's Future, 2010.

Christoff, Chris and Peggy Walsh-Sarnecki. "Michigan Education Association Has Plan: Get Teachers to Retire: Better Pensions for 9,000 Sought." *Detroit*

Free Press, January 28, 2009. http://istockanalyst.com/article/vewiStockNews/articleid/2988408 (accessed October 12, 2010).

Cichocki, Mikki. "Teacher Retirement Incentives + Merit Pay = Hmmm." February 21, 2010. http://www.mikki.com/2010/03/teacher-retirement-incentives-merit-pay-hmmm (accessed November 4, 2010).

CPS Human Resources. *Academy for Urban Leadership (AUSL): Turning Around Schools.* Chicago, IL: Chicago Public Schools Department of Human Resources, 2007.

Crosby, Sherry Joe, "Support System: Retired Teachers Team Up with New Ones." *The Free Library*, 1999. http://www.thefreelibrary.com/SUPPORT+SYSTEM%3B+RETIRED+TEACHERS+TEAM+UP+WITH+NEW+ONES.-a083625050 (accessed October 15, 2010).

Defense Activity for Non-Traditional Education Support (DANTES). "Current Status of Troops-to-Teachers." *Shift Colors* 47, no.4, July 1, 2005. http://www.dantes.doded.mil/dantes_web/troopstoteachers/index2.asp (accessed February 19, 2011).

Dillon, Sam. "With Turnovers High, Schools Fight for Teachers." *New York Times*, August 27, 2007. http://www.nytimes.com/2007/08/27/education/27teacher.html?sq=teacher.retention&st accessed November 12, 2010.

Dychtwald, Ken, Tamara J. Erickson, and Robert Morrison. *Workforce Crisis: How to Beat the Coming Shortage of Skills and Talents* (Boston, MA: Harvard Business School Press, 2006).

Edelsky, Carole, and Jenise Porter. "Teach for America: A Bad Deal for Public Education." *Queens Teacher.* August 16, 2010. http://queensteacher2.blogspot.com/2010/08/teach-for-america-bad-deal-for-public.html (accessed October 15, 2010).

Education4Excellence. "City Teachers Unveil Comprehensive Plan to Reform 'Last in-First out' Layoff Policy." http://www.educators4excellence.org/ (accessed March 1, 2011).

Fiarman, Sara Edith, Susan Moore Johnson, Mindy Sick Munger, John P. Papay, and Emily Kalejs Qazilbash. *Teachers Leading Teachers: The Experience of Peer Assistance and Review Consulting Teachers.* Cambridge, MA: Harvard Graduate School of Education, 2009.

Fibkins, William L. *An Administrator's Guide to Better Teacher Mentoring*, 2nd ed. Lanham, MD: Rowman and Littlefield, 2011.

————. "Why Am I Looking for Work When I Don't Have To?" In unpublished manuscript, The Dark and Sometimes Humorous Side of Retirement and Aging, 2009.

Foster, Elizabeth. "How Boomers Can Contribute to Student Success: Emerging Encore Career Opportunities in K-12 Education." *Civic Ventures*, 2010.

Freedman, Marc. *Encore: Finding Work That Matters in the Second Half of Life.* New York, NY: Perseus Books, 2008.

————. "The Selling of Retirement, and How We Bought It." *Washington Post*, February 6, 2005, B01.

Gabriel, Tripp. "Leader of Teachers' Union Urges Dismissal Overhaul." *New York Times*, February 25, 2011, A29.

————. "Teachers Wonder: Why the Scorn?" *New York Times*, March 2, 2011. http://www.nytimes.com/2011/03/03/education/03teacher.html?hp=&pagewanted=print (accessed March 3, 2011).

Gates, Bill. "How Teacher Development Could Revolutionize Our Schools." *Washington Post*, February 28, 2011. http://www.washingtonpost.com/wp-dyn/content/article/2011/02/27/AR2011022702876.html (accessed February 28, 2011).

Gordon, Gary. "Teachers Stick with Great Principals, Great Schools." *Gallup.com*, February 24, 2004. http://gallup.com/poll/10759/Teachers-Stick_Great-Principals-Great-Schools.aspx (accessed October 26, 2010).

———. "Teacher Retention Starts with Great Principals." *Gallup.com*, February 17, 2004. http://www.gallup.com/poll.10657/Teacher-Retention-Starts-Great-Principals.aspx (accessed October 26, 2010).

Gormley, Michael. "Poll: NYers Want Best Teachers Spared Layoffs." *Wall Street Journal*, February 24, 2011. http://www.wsj.com/article/AP2978a33501113419f8bd4965d8beede4.html accessed February 25, 2011.

Herszenhorn, David M. "Veteran Teachers in City Schools Help Colleagues Sharpen Skills." *New York Times*, November 1, 2004. http://nytimes.com/2004/11/01/education/01teach.html/sq=teacherretention&st+cs (accessed November 12, 2010).

Howell, Brandon. "Schools Offer Early Retirement Incentive." *Capital News Service*, April 16, 2010. http://capitalnewsservice.wordpress.com/2010/04/16/schools-offer-early-retirement-incentive (accessed November 10, 2010).

IBM. "Transition to Teaching: IBM Launches 'Transition to Teaching' Program." *IBM Gives News*, Fall 2008. http://ibm.com/ibm/ibmgivesnews/transition_to-eaching_shtml (accessed February 21, 2001).

Javier, Jeffrey. "Early Out for Peoria Unified Teachers." *Arizona Republic*, March 17, 2010. http://www.azcentral.com/commuity/peoria/articles/2010/03/17/20100317retirement-incentives-peoria-teachers.html (accessed November 4, 2010).

Johnson, Susan Moore, Jill Harrison Berg, and Morgaen L. Donaldson, *Who Stays in Teaching and Why: A Review of the Literature on Teacher Retention*. Cambridge, MA: Harvard Graduate School of Education, 2005.

Knight, Josh. "County Schools Consider Retirement Incentives." *WHSV.com*, February 24, 2010. http://gray.printthis.clickability.com/pt/cpt/action=cpt&title+County+Schools+consider+Retirement+Incentives (accessed November 4, 2010).

Kolata, Gina. "Taking Early Retirement May Retire Memory, Too." *New York Times*, October 12, 2010, D1.6.

Kossan, Pat. "Schools Offer Buyouts amid Teacher Shortage." *Arizona Republic*, September 2, 2006. http://www.azcentral.com/arizonarepoblic/news/articles/0902oaidoff0902.html (accessed October 12, 2010).

Lemmey, William. "Senior Teachers Are the Heart of the School." Letter to the Editor. *Newsday*, January 31, 2011, A22.

Lepper, Ruth. "Seven Teachers' Retirement End of an Era." *Sign On San Diego*, May 6, 2004. http://signonsandiego.printthis.clickability.com/pt/cot?action=cpt%title=Seven+teachers%2 (accessed September 1, 2010).

Light, Joe. "When the New Temp Happens to Be the Boss." *Wall Street Journal*, February 28, 2011. http://online.wsj.com/article/SB10001420527487046969290456716643324921455652.html.

Lopez, Tyler. "Budget Cuts Open Door for Some to Retire Early." *The Denver Channel*, April 10, 2010. http://www.thedenverchannel.com/print23106933/detail.html (accessed October 13, 2010).

124

Maeshiro, Karen. "Exit by Veteran Teachers? Districts Weigh Early Retirement Incentives." *The Free Library*. http://www.thefreelibrary.com/EXIT+BY+VETERAN+TEACHERS%3f+DISTRICTS+ (accessed November 10, 2010).

Math for America. "About MFA Fellows." http://mathforamerica.org/web/guest/about-us (accessed February 12, 2011).

Matthews, Karen. "NYC Unveils Teacher Layoff Plans." *Newsday*, March 2, 2011, A6, 7.

Milgrom-Elcott, Talia. *The Elusive Talent Strategy: An Excellent Teacher for Every Student in Every School*. A Carnegie Challenge Paper. New York, NY: The Carnegie Corporation of New York, 2011.

Miller, Mark. "Laid-Off Older Workers Face Multiple Obstacles." *Newsday*, March 5, 2011, B7.

———. "Our Graying Will Reshape the World." *Newsday*, February 19, 2011, B7.

Miller, Matt. "Buyouts, No Bailouts, for Teachers." *Washington Post*, May 11, 2010. http://www.washingtonpost.com/wp-dyn/content/article/2010/05/12/AR2010051202659 (accessed October 13, 2010).

Newport, Frank. "Americans' Projected Retirement Age Continues to Creep Up." *Gallup.com*, April 26, 2010. http://www.gallup.com/poll/127514/Americans-Projected-Retirement-Age-Continues-Creep-Up.aspx (accessed October 26, 2010).

Noguera, Pedro. "Reform Driven by Education Fads." *New York Times*, March 6, 2011. http://nytimes.com/roomfordebate/2011/03/06/why-blame-the-teachers/reform-drive (accessed March 7, 2011).

Noor, Moina. "Shortage of Principals Is Feared as Wave of Retirements Looms." *New York Times*, August 3, 2008. http://nytimes.com/2008/08/03/nyregion/nyregionspecial2/03principalsct.html (accessed November 21, 2010).

Novelli, Bill. *Fifty Plus: Give Meaning and Purpose to the Best Time of Your Life*. New York, NY: St. Martin's Press, 2008.

NYC Teaching Fellows. "Overview of NYC Teaching Fellows." http://nycteaching-fellows.org/program/overview.asp (accessed February 24, 2011).

O'Neil, Charles. "School District to Offer Teachers Early Retirement Initiative." *Harbor Light News*, April 21, 2010, accessed November 10, 2010, http://www.harborhightnews.com/af/php/sid=10145&current_edition-2010-04-21.

Posnick-Goodwin, Sherry. "Teacher Retirement on the Rise." *California Teacher Magazine*, June 2009. http://www.cta.org/Professional-Development/Publications?Educator-June-09/0609-action (accessed February 22, 2011).

Putnam, Molly. "What Politicians Don't Know." *New York Times*, March 6, 2011. http://www.nytimes.com/roomfordebate/2011/03/06/why-blame-the-teachers/what-politicians-don't-know (accessed March 7, 2011).

Rix, Sarah E. *Older Workers: Choice and Challenge*. Santa Barbara, CA: ABC-CLIO, Inc., 1990.

Rothwell, William J., Harvey I. Sterns, Diane Spokus, and Joel M. Reaser. *Working Longer: New Strategies for Managing, Training and Retaining Older Employees*. New York, NY: American Management Association, 2008.

Shea, Gordon F., and Adolf Hassen. *The Older Worker Advantage: Making the Most of Our Aging Workforce.* Westport, CT: Praeger Publishers, 2006.

Silverblatt, Bob. "Tracking the Recession: Buyouts Lure 9,000 Workers into Retirement." *Stateline.org,* August 18, 2009. http://stateline.org/live/details/story?contenId=418011 (accessed October 15, 2010).

Sloan Center on Aging and Work. "Older Adults Struggle in Job Search." *Sloan Center News,* November 16, 2010. http://www.bc.edu/research/agingandwork/all_feeds/2010/2010-11-16.html (accessed January 21, 2011).

Staley, Oliver. "Teacher Seniority Rules, Job Security, Threatened amid Budget Cuts." *Boston.com,* March 27, 2011. http://www.boston.com/nation/articles/2011/03/27/teacher_seniority_rules_job_security_threatened_amid_budget_cuts (accessed March 27, 2011).

Sustrin, Sheila, and Letty Sustrin. *The Teacher Who Would Not Retire.* West Bay Shore, NY: Blue Marlin Publications, 2002.

Teach for America. "How We Are Helping to Solve Educational Inequality." http://www.teachforamerica.org/what-we/do/our/approach (accessed February 20, 2011).

Texas Office of Aging Policy and Information. "Workforce and Older Texans." OAPI Policy Paper. Austin: Texas Office of Aging Policy and Information, 2002.

Toppo, Gregg. "Teach for America: Elite Corps or Costing Older Teachers Jobs?" *USA Today,* July 29, 2009. http://www.usatoday.com/news/education/2009-07-29-teach-for-america_N.htm (accessed October 15, 2010).

University of Texas. "About 70 Percent of New High School Principals Leave within Five Years, Study Says." *University of Texas at Austin News,* October 5, 2009. http://www.utexas.edu/news/2009/10/05/prncipalretention/ (accessed November 15, 2010).

Wilson, Rick. "121 Forest Hills Teachers, Staff Apply for Early Retirement Incentive." *Grand Rapids Press,* April 15, 2010. http://www.mlive.com/news/grand-rapids/index.ssf/2010/04/121_forest+hills-teacher_st (accessed November 10, 2010).

———. "Teacher Buyouts Could Prove to Be Too Popular for Michigan Schools." *Grand Rapids Press,* May 9, 2010. http://www.mlive.com/news/grand-rapids/index.ssf/2010/05/many_area_teachers_go_for_earl.html (accessed October 12, 2010).

Winerip, Michael. "A Chosen Few Are Teaching for America." *New York Times,* July 11, 2010. http://www.nytimes.com/2010/07/12/education/12winerip.html?.=&adxnnl=1&ref=teach_for_america&adxnnlx=1311778150-SoFuF84eRwtrAdIFQI2dIw (accessed October 16, 2010).

Yancey, Roy. "Taking Aim at Tenure in Teacher Layoffs." *Newsday,* March 2, 2011.

Zuboff, Shoshona, and James Maxmin. *The Support Economy: Why Corporations are Failing Individuals and the Next Episode of Capitalism.* New York, NY: Penguin Putnam, Inc., 2002.

About the Author

William Fibkins is an author and consultant. His focus is on education reform, teacher retraining and mentoring, intervention on behalf of at-risk students and parents, reorganizing school counseling programs, and establishing a "Circle of Wellness" in schools in order to address student health and wellness issues.

CPSIA information can be obtained at www.ICGtesting.com
Printed in the USA
BVOW071831271111

276942BV00001B/8/P